To my teacher
Chögyam Trungpa, Rinpoche

and to musicians and others
who long to express themselves from the heart

"Madeline Bruser has put together a valuable and insightful look at the art of practicing. If more people read this book, perhaps we might see an increase in the number of inspired and joyful music makers who, rather than viewing practice as a punitive activity, regard it as the supreme opportunity to explore their own creativity." —*American Music Teacher*

"Madeline Bruser gives us insight, wisdom, and tremendous practicality." —Don Campbell, author of *The Mozart Effect*

"I've often thought of practice as 'playing'—in the stretching, somersault, skipping, serenely special sense of the word—and *The Art of Practicing* reaffirms that. It gently and joyfully reminds us of the beautiful reasons we love music and become musicians in the first place." —Richard Stoltzman, clarinetist

"The attitude and approach presented in this book ring true and can inspire us to open up to music with stimulated imagination and inquisitiveness and to play 'from the heart' every time we sit down to play. I recommend this book and its ideas very highly." —Peter Serkin, pianist

"An excellent sourcebook for musicians . . . logical, well thought out, and clearly written, as well as medically tenable . . . thoughtful, sensitive, and very practical."
—Alice G. Brandfonbrenner, M.D., founding director,
Medical Program for Performing Artists,
Rehabilitation Institute of Chicago, and
editor, *Medical Problems of Performing Artists*

"This is a book to read and read again, whether you are a performing musician or a serious listener." —*Washington Times*

The Art of Practicing

A Guide to Making Music from the Heart

MADELINE BRUSER

BELL TOWER

New York

All the photographs in this book were taken by Allan Baillie. The photographs in
Figures 16, 17, 31, 32, 33, 47, 48, and 49 are courtesy Steinway Hall. The three
drawings are taken from *The Body Moveable* by David Gorman and modified by
William Conable in *How to Learn the Alexander Technique*. They are used by
permission.

Published by Bell Tower, an imprint of Harmony Books,
a division of Crown Publishers, Inc., 201 East 50th Street,
New York, New York, 10022. Member of the Crown Publishing Group.

Originally published in hardcover by Bell Tower in 1997.
First paperback edition published in 1999.

Random House, Inc. New York, Toronto, London, Sydney, Auckland

www.randomhouse.com

Bell Tower and colophon are trademarks of Crown Publishers, Inc.

Printed in the United States of America

This book is not intended as a substitute for the medical advice of physicians. Any
application of the recommendations set forth in this book is at the reader's
discretion and sole risk. The reader should regularly consult a doctor in matters
relating to health and particularly in respect to symptoms that may require
diagnosis or medical attention.

Book design by Susan Hood

Library of Congress Cataloging-in-Publication Date
Bruser, Madeline.
The art of practicing: making music from the heart/Madeline Bruser.
Includes bibliographical references and index.
1. Practicing (Music) 2. Music—Performance—Psychological aspects. 3. Music—
Performance—Physiological aspects. I. Title.
ML3838.B78 1997
781.44—dc21   96-45585

ISBN 0-609-80177-5

10 9 8 7 6 5 4 3 2 1

First Paperback Edition

Acknowledgments

Many people gave generously of their time, energy, and wisdom to bring this book into being.

I would like to thank my kind agent, John Thornton, who was the first to welcome me into the world of publishing. In addition to championing and selling this book, he skillfully edited each chapter. I am equally indebted to Toinette Lippe, dedicated editorial director of Bell Tower, who also welcomed me warmly. She allowed me to write in my own voice yet made just the right changes to polish the manuscript. My friend Joe Spieler, of the Spieler Agency, provided additional support and encouragement.

I am grateful to Lord Menuhin for his thoughtful foreword, and to the following musicians and teachers who, through generous interviews, provided valuable information on the use of the body: Stephen Burns, James Carson, Jeannette Lovetri, Frances Magnes, Melanie Nevis, Patrick O'Brien, Karen Ritscher, and Janet Weiss. I am equally grateful to the following health professionals, who gave valuable interviews as well: Dr. Fadi J. Bejjani; Dr. Patrick Fazzari; Caryl Johnson; Dr. Emil Pascarelli; Dr. Mark Seem; Deborah

Caplan, P.T.; Robert Cohen; Martha Eddy; Diane Nichols, M.S.W.; Joni Yecalsik; James Wang, P.T. (who also served as photo adviser for Chapter 3, "Stretching"); Hope Martin (who also edited Chapter 6, "Basic Mechanics," and was a photo adviser for that chapter); and Joan Campbell Whitacre (who also edited "Stretching" and "Basic Mechanics"). And special thanks to physicist David I. Caplan for his editing of "Basic Mechanics" as well.

Additional thanks to Arawana Hayashi, Wendy Hilton, Peter Lieberson, Andrew Mattison, Adam Rosenbloom, and Richard Sylvester for contributing to individual chapters.

Allan Baillie took the many fine photographs that appear in Chapters 3 and 6, and my good friend Rochelle Weithorn was stylist and makeup artist for the photographs. I am grateful to both of them for their expertise, generosity, and good spirits. I would also like to thank Erica vanderLinde Feidner, who arranged two photography sessions at Steinway Hall in New York with efficiency and care, and the entire Steinway Hall staff for their kind cooperation.

Special thanks to Irene Johansen, who prepared the musical examples and provided valuable editing for Chapter 11, "Spontaneous Insight." Thanks also to Sam Moore for his expert assistance with the musical examples and for helpful feedback on individual chapters.

Some of the "Questions and Answers" that appear in this book, as well as material in the main body of several chapters, are drawn from seminars arranged by the following people and institutions: Bruce Chapman and the Canadian Conservatory of Music; Marjorie Foxall and the Nova Scotia Registered Music Teachers Guild; Michael Meltzer, Peter Becker, and Leo Spellman from Steinway Hall; Michael Massaro and the Rockland County Music Teachers Guild; Joseph Gurt and the Music Department of Eastern Michigan University; and John Ankele and Current Production Group. Special thanks to the students and teachers whose wonderful questions appear in the book.

I am particularly indebted to writers Douglas Barasch, Ellen Perlman, and Barbara Stewart, who provided extensive editing of the proposal, believed in this book, and taught me the art of writing.

Judith Lief, Greg Morton, and Monica Stordeur also provided valuable editing, and Barbara Bash, David Bruser, Lawrence Bruser, Trish Burgess, Stephen Burns, James Carson, John Cheek, Allison DeSalvo, Bill Douglas, Mimi Dye, Richard Fields, Lillian Freundlich, Julie Gore, Steve Gorn, Ellen Green, Julie Leiter, Suzanne Macahilig, Bill McGaw, Mark Moffett, Robert Precht, Ted Riccardi, Karen Ritscher, and David Sable gave helpful feedback.

Thanks also to Carl Adams, Sharon Ascher, Richard Bishop, Dr. Alice Brandfonbrenner, William Conable, Clara Goetz, Elliot Jaeger, Jonathan Kramer, Michael Krugman, Peggy Levine, Caryll McGill, Jean Newstead, Joan Pfitzenmaier, Janice Ragland, Jessica Sarapoff, Amy Schwartzman, Judith Scott, Maureen Shannon, Shira Silverman, Andy Steigmeier, Roseanne Thom, Miu Tsang, Liang Wang, Dr. Frank Wilson, and Lydia Yohay.

I am grateful to my piano teachers for nurturing my talent and passing on their musical and pianistic knowledge: Priscilla Michael, Marcella Tonn, Jan de Jong, Alexander Libermann, Jeanne Stark-Iochmans, Menahem Pressler, Irwin Freundlich, Reginald Stewart, John Crown, Paul Hersh, and Nathan Schwartz. My thanks as well to the music schools at which I received valuable training and experience—Indiana University, the Juilliard School, the Music Academy of the West, the University of Southern California, and the San Francisco Conservatory of Music.

Many stories that appear in this book feature students who played in lessons, master classes, and workshops with me over the last several years. Their bravery, sincerity, and intelligence have contributed a great deal to the spirit and letter of this book.

I am grateful to Lee Cheek for her wonderful understanding and support and her helpful contributions, and to Betsy Capen for her valuable advice and warm encouragement.

I would especially like to thank my husband, Parlan McGaw, who lived with this book during its creation. He listened long and attentively to my ideas and my heart, helped me understand my own intentions more clearly, and provided much helpful advice. His love, support, and Promethean sense of humor nourished me throughout the writing. As if that weren't enough, he edited each chapter with insight and expertise.

Finally, I am profoundly indebted to Chögyam Trungpa, Rinpoche, master artist and meditation teacher, who presented the Shambhala and Buddhist teachings on which much of this book is based, and who personally instructed me in making music from the heart. Without him, I could never have begun this book. I hope that what I have written is true to his teaching and that it will give to the reader a small part of what he gave to me.

Contents

Contents

Part Three: Natural Command

Foreword

Madeline Bruser has much to contribute toward the practical, psychological, and spiritual approach to productive practicing. So often it is regarded as penance when it can be an exhilarating and rewarding effort. This book will contribute directly to this result.

More and more we realize that practicing is not forced labor; more and more we realize that it is a refined art that partakes of intuition, of inspiration, patience, elegance, clarity, balance, and, above all, the search for ever greater joy in movement and expression. This is what practice is really about.

Too many generations have been twisted into slavery and suffered the consequences of frustration, all manner of aches and pains, physical and spiritual, as well as mental depression. Ms. Bruser has the right approach, and I welcome this book.

Yehudi Menuhin

The Art of Practicing

Introduction

The word "practice" conjures up a variety of potent images and feelings. For some, it arouses dread and memories of long hours spent confined in a small room with a book of finger exercises and a metronome. Such practicing feels more like a punishment than a musical experience. For others, practicing is an escape from painful aspects of life—perhaps the only activity in which they feel free to express themselves. For the fortunate few, practicing is the overflow of joy and vibrant curiosity from a healthy and fulfilling life. Many of us recognize a little of ourselves in all of these descriptions. But whatever our experience is, all of us find practicing a constant challenge to our physical, mental, and emotional capabilities.

Every piece of music presents new difficulties, and each time we practice it new wrinkles appear. One day we may feel comfortable with our instrument, and the next we may feel stiff and uncoordinated. One minute a phrase flows smoothly from our fingers, and the next it suddenly falls apart. We are trying to turn a page of notes into a harmonious, pulsing, musical whole, and it takes all the sensitivity, intelligence, and precision we can muster. Along with the joy

1

of expanding our music-making capacities, we often experience tension and frustration. In many cases, the sheer physical strain from struggling for an ideal performance even leads to injury.

This book is about how to free ourselves from physical and emotional tension as we practice so that we can unleash our innate musical talent. When our fingers get tied up in knots in a difficult passage, we can loosen up and find a comfortable way to play it. When we're struggling to create a perfectly shaped phrase, we can stop to notice each sound and discover the subtleties we've been looking for. By giving ourselves room to relax, we awaken our vital energies instead of stifling them.

This book grew from seminars called "The Art of Practicing" that I began giving to musicians in 1985. My own work at the piano had changed radically in the late 1970s, when I started practicing mindfulness meditation. I tried meditation the day after an unsuccessful audition, thinking that it might help me be more relaxed and confident about performing. I was tired of having so much trouble sleeping the night before competing and of worrying so much about memory lapses. More important, although I had achieved a fair amount of success as a performer, I was dissatisfied with how I felt onstage. Something told me that a completely different kind of confidence must be possible, different from anything I had experienced before.

Meditation was simple. I sat still and focused on my breathing in order to develop an awareness of ordinary events in the present moment. This discipline slowed down my chattering, goal-oriented mind. I learned to relax, not worry so much about the past or the future, and perceive present events more clearly. In fact, I relaxed so much that I stopped practicing the piano altogether. I didn't know when, or even if, I would ever return to it. After two months, I was ready to come back. To my delight, my entire practicing experience was altered.

The relaxation and awareness cultivated during meditation spilled over into my work at the piano. I found myself taking half-minute breaks on the bench while practicing, no longer in a hurry to accomplish anything. It felt good just to sit there and take my time deciding what to do next. Subtleties I'd never noticed before—about the movement of my hands and the harmonies in the music—became striking and engaging. Gradually, I developed a new understanding of the physiological mechanics of playing. I also found that listening more attentively improved my physical coordination.

A whole new range of sounds came out of the piano—both a new gentleness and a more penetrating, forceful sound when the music needed it. The five inefficient hours a day that I used to put in at the piano were whittled down into three focused, productive hours. In short, I accomplished more with less effort, and with much more pleasure. My students tried the new techniques of moving, listening, and relaxing that I developed, and their playing improved dramatically, too. These techniques became the Art of Practicing.

From the first seminar I gave, I was struck by the hunger musicians have for guidance in their practicing. Beginning and advanced students, amateurs and professionals—all longed for a way to sustain their original inspiration while trying to meet the challenge of learning a great piece of music. Some had injured themselves by practicing improperly. Others simply felt uncomfortable with their instruments and frustrated by their inability to express themselves. Many were frightened and anxious about performing. They asked intelligent questions, and some of these, along with my answers, form a major part of this book.

The Art of Practicing is a step-by-step approach that integrates movement principles with meditative discipline, which consists of focusing on sounds, sensations, emotions, and thoughts in the present moment. It cultivates a clear and relaxed mind, an open heart, free and natural movement, and vivid, joyful listening. Both beginners and accomplished musicians can use this approach. In fact, meditative discipline nurtures a fresh, open state of mind called "beginner's mind," which is sometimes lacking in professionals, who bring years of habits to their work. I have enjoyed teaching beginners, as well as advanced students, because they have open minds. And I have often been struck by music coming through a beginner's fingers with more freshness, spontaneity, and pure expressiveness than many professionals have.

Part One of this book describes our common experience with the initial inspiration to make music and the ensuing struggle of practicing. Part Two presents the ten steps of the Art of Practicing, which are divided into four groups of techniques: preparatory steps, physical techniques, psychological techniques, and sensory and intellectual techniques. Part Three discusses performing as a natural outcome of healthy practicing.

Although I present the Art of Practicing as a series of steps that progress logically from one to the next, it is not necessary to follow these steps in strict, linear fashion. At certain moments during a practice session it may feel appropriate to jump forward or back one or more steps, and you may go through all the steps several times in one session.

In presenting this approach, my intention is to communicate what I know from my experience as a concert artist and teacher, a meditation instructor, and a student of movement. Above all, I wish to encourage musicians to trust their experience of their own bodies and minds, and to believe that within their struggle and confusion lie the passion and intelligence that are the keys to joyful, productive practicing and powerful performing.

PART ONE

The Starting Point

CHAPTER 1

Meeting Yourself

When one of my students was six years old he attended a piano recital by Arthur Rubinstein. The concert was sold out, and his seat was among many on the stage, just a few feet from the great pianist. With his father on one side of him and his piano teacher on the other, he sat transfixed throughout the performance. Fifty years later, he still remembers Rubinstein's face against the blackened auditorium, the angle of the lights falling on the stage, and the thunderous chords that opened the program. From the first sounds he heard, he immediately knew that for the rest of his life he would be bound in a powerful relationship with the piano.

Many musicians remember similar moments, when they first recognized the significance of music in their lives. My own memory is of sitting in the darkness of a concert hall as a child and staring up at the pianist on the stage. As he played, I knew that the magic emanating from the piano was not just something outside of myself, but that it was part of me. I felt that the spotlight shining on the performer was also shining into my heart, illuminating a musical world within me.

In these first perceptions of power and magic we meet ourselves as musicians. Whether you are five years old and irresistibly drawn to the piano in your home, or you are an adult who suddenly falls in love with music and decides to take lessons, the knowledge that you belong in the world of music is deep and indestructible. It is part of your basic nature, as much as the color of your eyes or the sound of your voice. Even your choice of instrument might feel choiceless; you hear a piano or a cello and somehow know that that is the instrument you must play.

A man with whom I went to music school began taking piano lessons when he was five. When he was eight, he heard a violin for the first time. He came home and told his parents, "If you don't buy me a violin I'm going to burn the piano." He is now a successful concert violinist.

When Rubinstein was three years old, he sat under the piano and watched his older sisters play. A year later, his parents presented him with a violin, thinking that the piano was a common instrument, unsuitable for his already obvious talents. He promptly broke the violin in half. Thus began an eighty-seven-year love affair with the piano that thrilled the world.

Such passion is familiar to us as musicians, whether we are amateurs or professionals. It is part of an unshakable confidence in our musicality. Yet no matter how confident we are, we feel vulnerable in the vast world of music and musicians. Children feel unaccomplished next to adults. Amateurs struggle with the belief that their musical sense is undeveloped compared to that of professionals. All of us know we need guidance in our musical journey. When we go to a teacher we hope that he or she will appreciate our sincerity of heart, and that the discipline we learn will enable us to express ourselves from the heart.

This vulnerability is healthy. Students worry that being

vulnerable means being open to attack and to destructive criticism from teachers. But vulnerable literally means "able to be wounded," which includes letting yourself be pierced emotionally by things. You feel so touched by a piece of music that it breaks your heart. A performer who feels penetrated by music in this way can communicate its power to the audience. A student who is vulnerable to her teacher can receive the warmth and encouragement she needs to grow. If you acknowledge and respect your vulnerability, you can choose to avoid destructive people, and to speak up when someone treats you improperly.

Vulnerability is the essence of being human and alive. A *New York Times* art critic once described several still-life paintings by saying the objects "lacked a sense of vulnerability and warmth, as if they had never been caressed by the painter's hand or eye." He seemed to imply that even these inanimate objects could come alive if handled with more gentleness and appreciation. I pictured a series of dull, lifeless fruits and bottles, needing to be seen as they really are, colorful and vibrant, and deserving the attention of a finer artist. This is our own need, to be known and appreciated for who we really are. It is this vulnerability that draws us to music, to the warmth and brilliance great composers share with us. Through their music, they touch us and bring out our tenderness and artistic intelligence.

Passion, confidence, and vulnerability are evidence of musical talent. If music were not in our blood, we wouldn't have such strong feelings. Countless times students ask, "Do you think I have talent? Do you think I'll be able to play well?" Each person's talent is unique, and some are more gifted than others, but an intense desire to play well indicates that music is already inside the person, pressing toward the surface and needing to come out. Know this, and take heart from it as you make your particular journey with music.

CHAPTER 2

Struggle and Freedom

Although we start out inspired to practice, sooner or later we begin to feel frustrated. We can't get the results we want, and we don't know why. We feel as though we are working too hard, yet it seems we must not be working hard enough. We start to doubt our ability. The piece that once felt fresh begins to feel stale.

Much frustration is caused by inefficient use of the body. Instrumental or vocal technique that goes against principles of healthy posture and movement creates unnecessary tension, which inhibits musical expression. (Chapter 6 will discuss posture and movement in depth.) Frequently, however, tension and inefficient technique stem from mental and emotional attitudes toward ourselves and our practicing.

One such attitude is that practicing is supposed to be repetitious and regimented—completely different from performing. When we perform, we are on the spot. Every moment feels charged with possibility. We are acutely aware of being in a wide-open space in which anything can happen. But when we practice, we box ourselves in. I have often thought how strange it is that I can be sitting at the piano in my own living room, completely alone and free to do anything I want, and yet fall into some habitual and unsatisfying way of working.

We don't know what to do with our freedom. We repeat passages in a joyless, desperate way to gain technical security. We adhere to a rigid plan for practicing a piece. We push ourselves to meet a deadline and feel inadequate when our work isn't going well. This severity, this habit of being hard on ourselves, destroys inspiration, making it difficult to develop the joy and spontaneity needed for performing. Recognizing this gulf between the joy of performing and the drudgery of practicing led me to develop the Art of Practicing.

The Art of Practicing is about art, about creating something fresh and genuine. In this approach, practicing is not so different from performing. Instead of practicing in a mechanical or programmed way, we practice being spontaneous. The spontaneity that marks a strong, communicative performance is actually cultivated during practice sessions. Although learning a piece necessitates repeating passages and going slowly rather than at concert tempo, the qualities of openness, uncertainty, freedom, and aliveness that characterize performing permeate practicing.

I first experienced this spontaneity in a practice room at music school. I had been practicing for several hours when I suddenly realized that the sound was coming directly out of the piano. Instead of singing the music in my mind, as I usually did, and focusing on that imaginary sound, I heard the actual sound. I was shocked by its vividness, and by the realization that although this brilliant sensory experience had been available to me for years, I had been missing it.

Perhaps you remember a moment when you heard a familiar chord and were unusually struck by its beauty. Or maybe you remember occasions when your movements suddenly became more free and natural than usual. This kind of receptiveness and ease does not have to be a rare event. It is something you can cultivate.

Listening and Producing

Everyone starts out in music as a listener. As young children, we hear music with freshness and delight. We fall in love with it and are entranced by the simplest song. But when we start practicing an instrument, we stop listening intently. We become so involved with producing sound that we forget to take it in. Instead of sitting back and enjoying the sound, as we would listening to a good concert or recording, we get caught up with trying to make the instrument do what we want, and trying to make the music sound as we think it should. In directing our attention toward these desired results, we take it away from the sound that could give us pleasure in the present moment.

This approach becomes a vicious circle. The less pleasure we receive, the more we try to force the instrument to give it to us, gripping it tightly instead of moving simply and comfortably. This excess tension impedes the flow of musical vibrations through the body, further reducing our responsiveness to sound. We thus deprive ourselves of the joy of full-bodied engagement with music.

Longing and Ambition

One of the Chinese symbols for the word "joy" also means "music." The pictograph shows two drums and a bell, on a stand:

This synonymy rings true with everyone who loves music. Even if a piece is extremely sad we feel joy in the ability to experience and express such powerful emotion. We have a profound need to share these feelings with other people, and such communication gives our lives meaning.

One of the greatest challenges of making music is to maintain some cool in the heat of our passion and joy. It is easy to become impatient when it takes us longer to learn a beautiful piece than we would like. We ache to get it in our fingers, our voice, our body, to make physical contact with the music we love. This longing is our greatest asset. It is our communicative energy. It is the raw, throbbing energy of the heart.

But longing is different from ambition. Longing is our innermost feeling about life. We yearn to connect to people, to music, to the world, and we know that every experience and every relationship, indeed life itself, inevitably ends. The opening of Mozart's G minor symphony is a powerful expression of such yearning. You can almost hear Mozart sobbing over life's beauty and transiency. Popular songs like "Imagine," by John Lennon, and "The Man I Love," by George Gershwin, also convey poignancy and longing. Sometimes, in the middle of a hectic day of shopping, I am stopped in my tracks by the sound of such a song coming over speakers in the store, melting my heart and helping me remember what life is about. Music satisfies our deep need to feel our longing heart, a core of softness in ourselves.

We lose touch with this heart when we become overly ambitious. Ambition is healthy, but it becomes destructive when we drive ourselves too hard. We become so anxious to get the result we want that we push our bodies and minds to do things before they are ready. Such striving might make us feel superficially good about ourselves, but it creates struggle and discomfort instead of ease and pleasure.

Struggle does not produce beautiful music. Music is such a

direct means of communication that the performer's state of mind is immediately transmitted to the listener. A pianist who looks as though he is slaving over a hot keyboard, hunching over and working very hard, creates a sense of claustrophobia. You can't breathe easily because he's so worked up. But a performer who walks calmly onto a stage, takes his time sitting down, and welcomes the opportunity to perform with relaxation makes you feel relaxed. When he plays with exhilaration and ease, you feel exhilarated and at ease.

Comfort, ease, and joy can be cultivated through practice. To do this, we must give up excessive ambition and the desperate struggle for results, and let ourselves feel the pain of our longing, of having to wait to make music the way we want to. We can learn to relax with this longing and to enjoy its soft, warm presence in the heart. This warmth will then shine through the music we make and touch the hearts of others. The techniques outlined in Part Two are designed to accomplish this relaxation.

I remember a particularly striking, spontaneous experience of letting go of ambition. I was making an audition tape in a recording studio. I had played the Chopin G minor ballade several times through and still wasn't satisfied. After the eighth take, my body felt drenched in pain from wanting to play it well. The engineer's voice came over the speakers like a death knell: "Ten minutes left." The piece was nine minutes long. I just gave up. I let myself completely feel the pain and played without trying so hard. To my amazement, my body relaxed, the pain dissolved, and the music sounded fluid and clear. It was the best take of the afternoon.

Receiving and Giving

Giving up our struggle opens us to the music. And the performer's job is to do just that—to open fully to music, to let it come in, physically and mentally, and to become an unobstructed channel for its transmission to other people. We cannot possibly give music to others without first receiving it ourselves. Practicing is the process of receiving what was written.

Receiving can be difficult. Many of us have grown up in environments that did not sufficiently encourage us to enjoy or appreciate ourselves. Yet we need such encouragement and warmth to stay receptive to our feelings and to music. I sometimes point out to students that their frustration with a piece is an indication that they care deeply about it. One student told me it was one of the most helpful things ever said to him. He was able to stop berating himself and began to appreciate himself instead, which opened him up enormously to the music. We don't usually use experiences of dissatisfaction as signals to be gentle with ourselves. Instead, we blame ourselves or become aggressive with the music. Tension escalates, and the more we practice a piece, the worse it gets.

Ways of Struggling

Musicians create tension in a variety of ways. One of the most common is trying to play a piece fast before you are ready. When you push your body to move fast, it tightens, which only prevents it from moving as fast as you want it to. Even if you are worried about meeting a deadline, take your time.

Another misguided approach is to try to play something pianissimo or fortissimo when you are just beginning to learn it, and when the nervous system is not yet ready to do that; it's too difficult. You try so hard to play softly that you produce either a tight sound or no sound at all; or you force yourself to play loudly, which makes your muscles clench and become rigid, leaching their power and creating a strained sound. It is similar to what happens if you grip the front of your neck with your hand and then try to talk or sing: The physical constriction limits sound production. If, instead, you simply play comfortably, the required softness or loudness will come naturally with time.

Tension also comes from trying to manufacture a special kind of energy, particularly if a piece is romantic or emotional. You think, "Chopin was in a fever when he wrote this, so I'm going to produce a big fever." You get worked up and heavy, huffing and puffing, which is exhausting. Or you think, "Beethoven was an angry person, so I should get angry in order to play this piece." When you force emotion that way, you become tight, and the composer's power cannot flow through your body. Fierce energy comes through when the body is loose and free.

A particularly dangerous form of struggle is practicing through physical pain. Some musicians feel it is necessary to experience muscle soreness, as if they were pumping iron, when working hard to develop technique. This is a completely false notion. Pain is an indication that you are overusing a limited muscle group, using the wrong muscles, or using too much force. It is a signal to relax and slow down. At some point your body reaches a limit. The pain builds up until it becomes incapacitating. Injuries of the hands, arms, neck, back, jaw, lips, or vocal cords afflict many musicians, forcing them to stop playing or singing for extended periods of time, and sometimes permanently. One of the most well known examples is pianist Leon Fleisher, whose celebrated international career came to an abrupt halt when his right hand stopped functioning properly. Looking back on the torturous practicing that caused this tragedy, Fleisher commented, "There was something macho about practicing *through* the pain barrier. Even when my hand was exhausted, I kept going. Although I thought I was building up muscle, I was, in fact, unraveling it."[1]

The tendency to drive oneself physically leads some musicians to rely heavily on finger exercises to improve their technique. One student spoke about spending hours practicing exercises by Phillip or Pischna. "Your muscles can ache," she said, "and the exercises aren't interesting. But don't they strengthen you?" The value of an exercise depends on your state of mind. If you don't find it interesting, then it is not useful. Muscular pain is not necessary, and muscle power is not as important as good coordination. If you are genuinely interested in the technical concept of a particular exercise and you listen well and move comfortably, you can learn a great deal about your body, and it can be enjoyable and helpful.

I myself have rarely done exercises. An exercise is simply a series of notes taken out of normal musical context, and usually sequenced and repeated. Many written exercises are lengthy and unmusical, and practicing them can easily become tedious. Concert pieces like Chopin études, on the other hand, are interesting to practice because each solution to a technical difficulty yields an appealing musical effect. One of my teachers had a wonderful analogy for using real music instead of exercises to develop technique. If he wanted to exercise his legs, he said, he wouldn't pace around his room; he would go for a walk in the park, where he could enjoy the fresh air, the trees and flowers and birds, and maybe even see some pretty women. Practicing exercises you don't enjoy is confining and saps your energy, whereas practicing a difficult but beautiful piece of music *gives* you energy. We feel revitalized by music, and we need that.

Psychotherapist Diane Nichols, director of the Performing Arts Psychotherapy Center in New York, says musicians are harder on themselves than dancers or actors, and have a more difficult time with their work. This is partly because musicians work primarily alone, and when they eventually play for an audience it is overwhelming. Also, performing music requires extreme precision. If your finger moves an eighth of an inch in the wrong direction, people can tell you have made a mistake. Because of the need for this precision, musicians are also more susceptible to noticeable memory lapses than other performers. They are afraid of "blanking out" or making blunders in front of an audience.

The fear of not being perfect drives musicians to overpractice and practice without joy. I remember being in music school and walking around looking through the little windows in the doors of the practice rooms. In every room a student was going full steam at his or her instrument, without stopping, like a locomotive. Rarely did anyone allow a minute's pause for reflection or relaxation, for maybe turning the page and seeing what was ahead. If someone did stop practicing for a minute, he may have heard a student in the next room playing the same piece at a faster tempo. One of my classmates discovered that another piano student deliberately tried to make him feel bad by playing the same repertoire faster and louder in a practice room near his.

This intense perfectionism and competitiveness sometimes causes musicians to develop an incapacitating tension that doctors call "overuse syndrome." Even if they have a good technique and are not repeating the same passages excessively, they overuse their technique. Afraid of not practicing enough, they injure themselves by practicing too much.

Trusting Ourselves

All of these ways of practicing indicate lack of trust in our ability. We are afraid that if we just relax and let ourselves work naturally and comfortably, we won't be good enough. So we drive ourselves, force ourselves, and hurt ourselves. In doing so, we lose touch with our most valuable asset as artists—the willingness to be vulnerable, genuine, and spontaneous, to communicate from the heart.

Communicating this openly in performance feels risky. You are on the spot and can't control what will happen. But it is invigorating because you are wide awake to the present moment. You walk onto the stage and notice every little thing—how your shoe feels on your foot, how the light hits the floor, how the shadows fall, every little sound in the audience. You think, "Oh, no! I don't know if I can do this! All these things are going on!" These things are going on every day, all day in your life, yet suddenly you are aware of them. As you place your fingers on your instrument or open your mouth to sing, you feel extraordinarily sensitive to every move you make.

The Art of Practicing is a discipline that cultivates this heightened awareness in every moment of our practicing. We practice noticing the details of our sensory experience, letting the sensations of sound, touch, and movement saturate the body and mind from moment to moment. By deliberately practicing such receptiveness, we gradually become familiar with the experience of brilliant awareness, and we begin to feel at home in the bright light on stage.

QUESTIONS AND ANSWERS

Question: *I feel I have a long way to go in being able to play things fast, and that if I don't push myself I'll never make it. How can I relax and trust myself if I really don't know if I have what it takes?*

Answer: Speed develops when the body is functioning comfortably, with minimum tension, so speed can come only if you don't push yourself. It's true you never know if you can accomplish something that seems far in the future, and each person has a different innate capacity for finger dexterity and speed. Nevertheless, you can't get somewhere without making the journey.

Speed is different from rushing. I saw a movie about Arthur Rubinstein in which he sat very simply and played without any sense of hurry whatsoever. Even playing a difficult piece, like the Chopin F minor concerto, he looked totally comfortable, and the notes came simply, one after another, with plenty of speed but with a tremendous sense of relaxation and freedom.

We have to continually remind ourselves to take our time, because we are usually impatient. We want results. Slowing down doesn't have to feel like holding back. It can be an opportunity to revel in sounds and sensations, to not be so concerned about where we are going but to enjoy the moment and become comfortable where we are.

Speed will come. If you play the same passage ten times without trying to get faster, it will get faster anyway. If you turn a metronome on the first time you play it and the last time, it will be faster the last time. It's a natural process, like discovering you can run after you've learned to walk.

You can't develop your potential by trying to be somebody else. You have to start with what you have. Then things can open up. The body works well when you treat it gently.

Question: *I don't understand how you can be spontaneous when you practice. If the way you practice determines how you will perform, then shouldn't you be very careful about how you practice?*
Answer: Yes, but not too careful, because then you don't have room to be yourself. You can be careful with the music without walking on eggs, which limits your freedom, physically and mentally. You tighten up, so you can't express yourself fully.

Q: *But I read that the pianist Czerny suggested trying to practice something ten times consecutively without making any mistakes as a way to prepare for a performance. Is that a good idea?*

A: That's too rigid. A better idea would be to practice performing for people and to become accustomed to making mistakes. Then you'll be ready, because, after all, constant, absolute technical perfection is humanly impossible. It's good to get used to that fact.

Being note-perfect is not the point. Of course it's nice if you can play every single note at the right time. But making music involves a lot more than that; otherwise a machine could do it. You can't express yourself genuinely if you're trying too hard not to make mistakes. You have to be willing to stumble over your words occasionally when you talk to people, so that something spontaneous can happen. Making music is the same way. Artur Schnabel made more mistakes than many pianists, but people usually didn't mind. He touched his audience deeply because he was spontaneous. He had something to say and allowed himself to say it.

People often think that you can't be precise and relaxed at the same time, but with the kind of discipline I'm suggesting, precision and relaxation come together. Because you are relaxed, you are free to move easily and to express yourself clearly. So you actually make fewer mistakes.

Question: *I thought finger exercises were a necessary part of learning an instrument. How can we develop technique without them?*

Answer: Musical compositions, along with simple scales, provide plenty of opportunities to develop technique. But some people prefer to use exercises to focus on a particular technique. That way, when they encounter the same technical demand in a composition, they are free to enjoy the music more and to focus on technique less. Other people, myself included, prefer to spend all of their practice time on real music, even if it means isolating a difficult passage and working with it extensively as if it were an exercise. In any case, technically challenging repertoire always requires that type of practice. Do what is most enjoyable for you.

Question: *How do you motivate a student to work harder without making her tense?*

Answer: The key is "healthy" or "relaxed" effort: neither too tight nor too loose, too tense or too lazy, but finding the proper balance between these extremes. It takes effort to move your arm, but it can be done naturally and comfortably. You can use your mind in the same way. You don't have to force yourself to race through your practice session. If a student begins to practice in this relaxed way, she enjoys it more, and her motivation develops naturally.

Question: *I've never felt a hundred percent prepared for a performance, so I don't understand how it's possible to overpractice. Isn't it true that you can never practice enough?*

Answer: It depends on what you mean by "prepared." A hundred percent preparation is impossible, because every piece of music has an infinite number of facets; you can always do more. So you prepare as much as time allows. People very often overpractice. I find that if I rest more and practice less I usually play better. Overpracticing comes from fear, which locks the mind and body and limits your spontaneity. Overdoing it also makes you physically tense and exhausted. Musicians usually wish they had more time to prepare—just a couple more days, or a week—before their performance. But when the moment of performance comes, you have to abandon your idealism in order to express yourself freely.

Question: *If you're open in the way you describe, can you be receptive to a piece that you're not strongly attracted to?*

Answer: The ideal situation is to love the piece that you're playing. Then expressing yourself comes more naturally, and you have more to give an audience. We all have our particular affinities. But professional musicians often have to perform a piece they don't feel passionate about. Accompanists play repertoire chosen by the soloist. Competitions frequently require certain pieces; so do teachers. A soloist might have an opportunity to play with an orchestra if he is willing to play a particular concerto.

If you try to be receptive to a piece you don't love, you can expand your emotional range and grow as a musician. Without an initial passion for the music, your performance may be somewhat limited. It may be that the piece is limited. Or a piece may not suit your temperament or personal style. But it's important to expand your musical and emotional range as much as possible, especially when you're young. Later on, it's important to recognize your strengths, and not to think you're inferior or inadequate as a musician just because you have certain affinities.

Question: *It's hard to find my own pace at music school because the environment is geared to working fast. How do we avoid getting caught up in that rush and competitiveness?*

Answer: A lot is expected of music students. When I was in school I often felt that the pace went against my grain. But a musician-in-training must become familiar with a wide variety of musical styles and a lot of repertoire. Teachers sometimes assign a new piece every week. This is particularly difficult when other students are able to learn pieces quickly and you have to compete with them. Or maybe you can learn a piece quickly, but you don't enjoy doing so because you have no time to study it in depth.

The school is trying to prepare students for the realities of the profession. Sometimes you are asked to perform a piece on short notice, or your manager may want you to know two or three dozen concertos so he can book you for a lot of concerts. Nevertheless, some very successful performers have small repertoires. They just know what they do best, and that's what they present to the public.

When you're in your twenties, you find out who you are as an artist—which composers you prefer and which music suits your voice. Let your teacher introduce you to a wide variety of music, and take time to search for new repertoire on your own. Maybe you will discover pieces that inspire you more and still provide the same challenges. If you feel the requirements are too demanding, discuss your feelings with your teacher. Don't be afraid to request a slightly lighter load, and explain that you'd like to try to produce higher quality work by concentrating on fewer pieces.

When you feel overwhelmed by how much you have to do, take a few moments to remember your love for the music, and let yourself enjoy it as much as you can.

Question: *Many musicians I know have developed injuries, and I've become so afraid of getting one myself that my body tightens up now when I practice. I know I need to relax in order to avoid hurting myself, but it's as though I'm afraid that if I move my hands and arms I'll do something wrong. How can I let go of this tension?*

Answer: It can be hard to relax in the climate of fear and competitiveness that surrounds a young performer. Contractors don't usually hire a freelance player who has had an injury even after he's recovered from it. As a result, many musicians choose to hide the fact that they're suffering from tension or pain until it disables them. So it's a vicious circle of pain and fear. As awareness of the prevalence of injury and its causes and cures increases in the musical profession, prejudice against the formerly injured is gradually decreasing. Unfortunately, funding of orchestras has also decreased, making jobs extremely difficult to get, even for those who have never been hurt.

Learning about how your body works and sharing your concerns with people you trust can help you deal with the fear and confusion surrounding pain and injury. It is especially important to be kind to yourself when you notice you are tightening up. Your fear is understandable, and the better you understand it, the less grip it will have on you. Ask yourself what exactly you are afraid of. You may be afraid that you will hurt yourself so badly that you will never play again. Or you may be afraid that an injury would ruin your chances for a job or competition. Whatever your fear is about, it has a lot to do with how much you love music and how much you long to express yourself as an artist and person. Appreciating these healthy feelings and desires can help you relax and let go. It can also help you be a good friend to others who are scared. The more understanding and kindness we can develop toward those who have been injured, the more everyone will be able to communicate openly about practice-related ailments, receive help when they need it, and learn how to avoid hurting themselves in the future.

PART TWO

A Ten-Step Approach

CHAPTER 3

Stretching

Step One: Stretch.

On the day of a concert, performers instinctively take good care of themselves. We rest, eat good food, avoid stressful activities, and generally do everything possible to relax and energize ourselves for making music. We know that to perform well we need to feel healthy, emotionally balanced, and confident. If we are tense, exhausted, or upset, we can't express ourselves fully.

Backstage we take deep breaths or stretch to relax and loosen up. We may sit quietly to focus the mind or converse with stagehands or other performers to open up emotionally. Some performers eat a favorite high-protein breakfast that day; some drink fruit juice right before performing to combat low blood sugar caused by nervous excitement. Whatever routine or ritual we follow, we are more conscious than usual of what we are doing and why.

We seldom take such care before practicing. We typically approach our instrument in come-as-you-are fashion, carrying a load of physical tension and mental clutter. Whether we resent having to practice or we are eager to connect to the music and anxious to accomplish something, we don't take time to calm down, collect ourselves, and ease into our work.

Practicing is a chance to be with the music you love. You can bring your best to it or you can cheat yourself of the opportunity to discover the depths of the music and of your own gifts. Your body, mind, heart, and sense perceptions are your gifts. If you use them properly, they will serve you well. The Art of Practicing begins with three steps that prepare you physically, mentally, and emotionally for making music.

Step One is *Stretch*. Students often arrive at my studio in a frazzled state. They have spent hours at school or work, and they have just come from noisy city streets. They need to unwind and decompress; their bodies look as though they've been scrunched up in a can all day with the lid on. They need to remove the lid, jump out, and revitalize themselves so they can approach the piano with ease and sensitivity.

Stretching takes out the kinks and lets the body breathe. Many of my students begin every lesson with a few minutes of stretching. As they let go of accumulated tension, they visibly escape from their compressed, "canned" state and expand into human beings with flexible limbs, juices flowing freely again.

Health professionals find that musicians tend to be sedentary and out of shape. Even two minutes of stretching works wonders by circulating blood and oxygen to thirsty tissues throughout the body. No matter what your instrument is, the energy of your whole body flows into the instrument to create the sound. Body energy is self energy, and when you let it come out, you express yourself.

When fresh blood and oxygen aren't pumping freely through the body tissues, the muscles get tired and don't function well. Energy is low instead of ready-to-go. Stretching releases tense muscles, preparing them for work. Some health professionals advise stretching the muscles you use for playing your instrument both before and after practicing. The forearms and shoulders of many musicians get a workout every day; stretching conditions them for and refreshes them after the steady stream of contractions they perform. If you feel particularly stiff in these areas, a physical therapist can recommend specific stretches to suit your needs.

Stretching the back is particularly important. The muscles in the posterior of the body—the back itself, the back of the neck, the buttocks, and the backs of the legs—tend to be cramped from daily activities. These muscles hold us upright against the force of gravity, and stretching them prepares them for this major task.

Loosening the spine frees up the spinal cord and its attaching sensory and motor nerves. The cord runs through the vertebrae, and its attached nerves emerge through openings in the sides of the vertebrae. Tight muscles and connective tissue can compress the spinal column and partially block the outlets from the vertebral openings. Sensory perception depends on the aliveness of the sensory nerves, while motor action depends on the readiness of the motor nerves. Since stretching the spine can free up the spinal nerves that lead to both the sense organs and the muscles, it can increase sensitivity to sounds and sensations and increase motility of the muscles.

My friend Joan Campbell Whitacre, a wonderful movement teacher, says that physical activity, beyond the limited movements of playing your instrument, is essential to musical sensitivity: "To the extent that we don't move, we cut off our ability to perceive and to feel. When tissues are inactive or tense, their sensory ability diminishes. The nerve endings are not receiving an adequate amount of stimulation."

In addition to awakening the sensory system, stretching circulates oxygen to the brain, allowing us to think clearly. Office workers who sit in one position for extended periods of time benefit from periodic stretch breaks. So do musicians.

Finally, if you breathe fully while you stretch, the movement of the breath makes the space inside the body more fluid so that the organs can expand and move more freely. Musical vibrations can then move more easily through the organs, bringing you into a more complete engagement with the music as you play or sing. You literally create a more full-bodied tone.

The stretches illustrated in this chapter are designed primarily to limber up the back, neck, shoulders, and forearms, as well as to increase general circulation. To get a feeling for how effective these stretches are, practice your instrument for a few minutes without stretching and then again after stretching.

How to Stretch Safely and Effectively

Stretching is best done when the body is warmed up from a hot bath or shower, or from light exercise, such as a three-minute walk. If you stretch with cold, stiff muscles, you can strain them instead of loosening them up.[1] One way to warm up your body is to lie on the floor with your arms and legs extended up toward the ceiling, shake them out, and continue moving all the joints of your limbs through their full range of motion in different directions. In this position the joints can warm up without taking on the weight of the body.[2] Or, you can stand and shake out your limbs; let each arm and leg shake and flop around as if you were a rag doll. Let your neck and spine get into the act and loosely shake your whole body.

To be most effective, stretches should be slow, gentle, and prolonged. Moving too fast can strain a muscle or a joint.[3]

Don't bounce back and forth to the stretched position. This "ballistic" bouncing aggravates muscle tissue and can cause injury.[4] Instead, ease into the stretch, relax, and breathe to allow muscles to release.[5]

Wear loose clothing or loosen your belt and collar so that you can move freely. If possible, take off your shoes. As you relax into each stretch, let yourself breathe fully and notice how the stretch affects your body when you exhale.

Joan Campbell Whitacre suggests coordinating your breathing with the stretching in the following manner: "Initiate the stretch as you begin an exhalation. Continue breathing and stretch only as far as the tissues are willing to go; don't force the tissues to stretch. When you get to a point of discomfort or stiffness, see if you're able to relax with it by deepening each inhalation and extending each exhalation. If you can continue to give in and experience a release of the discomfort, you're on the right track." Don't do a stretch if it hurts or if it feels wrong for your body. If you feel increasing pain instead of a release in tension, gently ease out of the position.

The stretches illustrated in this chapter are performed by yoga teacher Joni Yecalsik. Don't try to force your body into a position that feels extreme for you; just stretch as far as you comfortably can. When doing stretches #1, 2, 4, and 5, it is calming for the brain and nervous system to have the forehead supported. If you are not limber enough for your head to have contact with your legs or the floor, you can use pillows or a chair seat to support it.

With the exception of #9, hold each stretch for 5 to 60 seconds, depending on what is comfortable for you and on how much time you have. If you're a beginner or an older person, you may not feel ready at first to stay in any of these positions for a long time. Be gentle with your body. As with any exercise program, check with your doctor or physical therapist before you attempt these stretches.

Thirteen Stretches

1. Forward Bend: Sit on the floor with the soles of your feet together. Slowly bend forward with your arms stretched out in front of you and the palms of your hands on the floor. Let your head drop as far as it will go. Relax your arms and your entire body.

2. Side Stretch: Sit with legs apart, and stretch your arms toward your right foot. Let your head drop as far as it will go. Keep your knees unlocked, and relax your body. Repeat, stretching your arms toward your left foot.

3. The Plow: Sitting on the floor, roll backward from your hips so that your legs extend over your head and your feet touch the floor. (If they don't yet reach the floor, fill in the space with pillows or a chair seat to help you balance and relax.) Let your arms rest on the floor at your sides.

4. Backstretch 1 and 2: (1) Coming out of the plow, roll forward and extend your legs in front of you. Place your hands loosely around your knees and extend your elbows to the side. Let your head drop; keep your knees unlocked. Notice how your back and hamstrings feel. (2) Repeat, but this time place your hands around your calves instead of your knees; keep your elbows extended out to the side. Notice how this position stretches your back slightly differently.

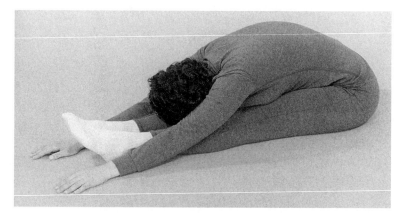

5. Backstretch 3: Sit on the floor with your legs straight ahead. Extend your arms in front of you with the palms of your hands on the floor. Drop your head and keep your knees unlocked. Notice how your back feels.

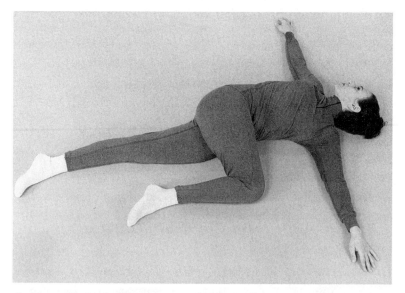

6. Knee Spiral: Lie on your back with your arms stretched out to the side. Bend your right knee and drop it over your left leg toward the floor. Turn your head to the right. Repeat with the left knee over the right leg, and the head turned to the left.

7. Forward Bend, Standing: Stand with your feet hip-width apart and slowly bend forward, letting your head and hands drop as far as they will go. Don't lock your knees.

8. Standing Twist: Bending forward, place your right hand loosely around the inside of your right knee with your elbow out to the side. Stretch your left arm up toward the ceiling and turn your head to the left, trying to see the back of your left hand. Don't lock your knees. Repeat with your left hand inside your left knee and your right arm extended upward.

9. Side-to-Side Twist: With legs shoulder width apart and arms stretched out to the side, gently twist your upper body back and forth from right to left.

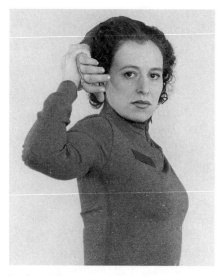

10. Neck and Shoulder Stretch: Clasp your left wrist with your right hand and hold it in back of your head. Pull your arms to the right and then to the left.

11. Arm Twist: Cross your right arm over your left at the elbow in front of your body. Move your two forearms toward each other and press your left fingers against your right palm. Close your right hand. Repeat with arms and hands reversed.

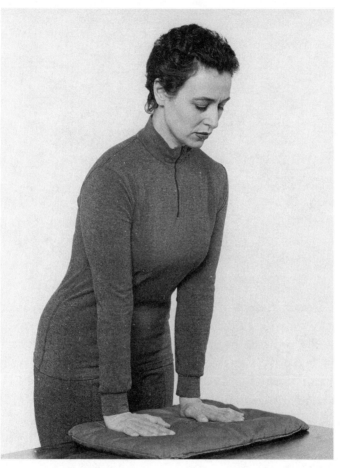

12. Forearm Flexor Stretch: Place a cushion or folded towel on a table in front of you. Place the palms of your hands on the padded surface with your fingers pointing away from you. Let your fingers relax; don't spread them uncomfortably apart. Straighten your arms, and lean your body slightly forward, *without leaning your weight on your hands.*

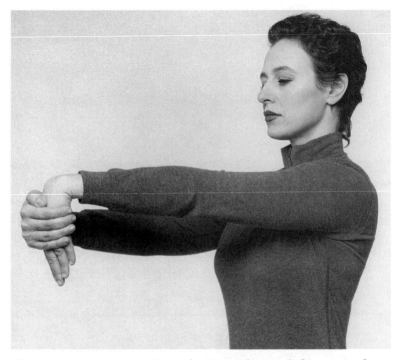

13. Forearm Extensor Stretch: Extend your left arm in front of you with your elbow straight. Let your hand drop from the wrist. Place the palm of your right hand against the back of your left hand *above the fingers;* with the right hand, pull the left hand toward you to bend the left wrist farther. Repeat with hands reversed.

If you know other stretches that you enjoy doing, feel free to add them to these, or do some of these and some of your own. Listen to your body, and do what feels good.

You can also stretch for a couple of minutes in the middle of a practice session if you feel stiff or tight. It will loosen you up and get your energy flowing freely again.

QUESTIONS AND ANSWERS

Question: *Do you recommend getting regular exercise, like running or working out, in addition to doing these stretches?*
Answer: Yes. Swimming is the safest exercise because it doesn't jar your joints. Several years ago I started swimming regularly, and now I can't imagine living without it. In addition to toning up the muscles and increasing your breathing capacity and cardiovascular strength, vigorous exercise also produces endorphins, resulting in a lift in your mood.

Swimming strengthens the shoulder muscles. Strong shoulders and upper arms take some of the load off the forearms, which are pushed to the limit in playing many instruments. Health professionals often advise instrumentalists to avoid lifting weights to strengthen their arms, because using the hands to grip heavy objects is antithetical to the delicate muscular control a musician needs. On two occasions a student has come to a lesson with me with unusually tight arms from lifting weights during the week. If you want to strengthen your shoulders and upper arms, you can use weights that strap onto your wrist or upper arm, and increase the amount of weight slowly. You can buy strap-on weights at sporting goods stores, and a professional trainer, physical therapist, or movement therapist can teach you how to use them properly.

Yoga, properly taught, provides both a workout and a release of tension. Teachers of Iyengar yoga, in particular, adapt yoga poses to the needs of individual students. If you are stiff, you become more flexible; if you lack strength, you learn to balance flexibility with strength. This method is especially helpful if you have an injury because it trains you to use your muscles to support your joints, helping you to avoid pain and to recover from the injury.

CHAPTER 4

Settling In

Step Two: Settle down in your environment.

I remember sitting in the balcony of Avery Fisher Hall and watching Yehudi Menuhin walk onstage to conduct an orchestra. He entered slowly and quietly, and I was immediately overtaken by his regal presence. As he stepped onto the podium, acknowledged the applause, and raised his baton, his body seemed poised to produce a performance that was already fully alive inside him. Maintaining a majestic steadiness in his posture as he conducted, he made only simple, gentle movement with his arms, yet each gesture commanded an exquisite wave of sound from the orchestra. When the concert was over, I went backstage to meet him and was surprised to find that this man of towering presence was shorter than I was.

What I perceived in him onstage was an inner stillness; in front of three thousand people and in the midst of torrential musical events, he was at home. It was as though he never forgot the silence from which all the sound arose and to which it would return. This inner stillness, this ability to be steady and to accommodate the most dynamic play of energies, is at the core of that prized commodity we call presence.

Steadiness allows a performer to master the complex mix of emotions in music rather than being thrown off balance by one emotion and left unready for the next. You can see this quality even in the most bravura instrumental playing. In a filmed performance of the Elgar Cello Concerto, Jacqueline du Pré handles vigorous, rapid passages with aplomb, returning after each series of dramatic sweeps of the bow to a state of complete composure. She continually dives into the music with exuberance and abandon, yet she projects an arresting natural dignity throughout her performance.

We imagine that Jacqueline du Pré had great presence even when she was practicing. Yet we think that presence is not something we can practice; we either have it or we don't. Few of us are as gifted as Yehudi Menuhin or Jacqueline du Pré; such phenomenally talented performers naturally exude a magnetic musical vitality and warmth. But we *can* cultivate our *own* presence. We can bring more of ourselves, more inner strength and conviction, to practicing than we usually do. Through proper training, we can discover powers within us that we didn't know we had. This chapter and the next offer techniques for doing that.

Being Present

Presence is the state of being fully present, of body, mind, heart, and sense perceptions being completely engaged with the activity of the present moment. For a performer, this means not only being engaged with the music but letting the energy of the audience affect you. In practicing, it means being at ease in your surroundings and being aware of each movement and each sound that you make.

Presence begins with a mind that is wide awake. After a good vacation our mind is fresh and alert, and we feel ready to plunge into practicing. Our technique might be a little rusty, but we are fascinated with the details of movement, fingering, and phrasing. In the middle of a stressful day, however, when the mind is filled with ten thousand things, or with a running commentary on how we should have said such-and-such yesterday to so-and-so, we can hardly even respond to the notes on the page. The body is present, but the mind is somewhere else. We need a reliable way of emptying the mind of clutter so we can take in what's in front of us.

A practice called "mindfulness of breathing" has recently become widely recognized as a highly effective method for clearing the mind and relaxing the body. Discovered in ancient times by Shakyamuni Buddha as a form of meditation, this simple practice of focusing on the breath has immediate and profound beneficial effects. Heart specialists teach it to patients to help them lower their blood pressure. People suffering from severe injuries use it to ease their pain. This is the technique used to accomplish *Step Two: Settle down in your environment.*

Posture

Upright posture is important for this breathing exercise because it allows the lungs to function easily. To begin, sit on a firm seat (which could be the chair or bench you use when playing your instrument), comfortably upright, letting your torso rest naturally on your sit bones. The sit bones are the two bones at the base of the pelvis; you can feel them when you shift your weight from side to side. These bones are designed to be sat on; we balanced easily on them as babies, just sitting on the floor. But as we got older, we got used to slouching in chairs, and we lost the habit of sitting in an uplifted way. (Chapter 6, "Basic Mechanics," will discuss posture in detail.)

With your feet solidly on the floor, your hands resting on your thighs, and your head up and facing forward, let your gaze drop to a comfortable level—about 45 degrees down. Don't try to focus on what's in front of you; let your eyes relax. Let your jaw relax as well. You can open your mouth a little if it helps you breathe more easily.

Mentally scan your body from head to toe to notice places where you're tense. Consciously let the muscles relax. Many actors are trained in this method of loosening up before walking onstage; letting go of tension frees up their vital energies for performing.

Breathing

After assuming this posture, place your attention on your breath as you exhale. Just notice it. You don't need to pay any particular attention as the breath comes in, just as it goes out. And you don't need to breathe in any special way; just let the breath be as it is. Do this for at least two minutes. If you're reading this in a quiet place, do it now, before reading further.

Breathing out is very relaxing. Usually we don't let ourselves exhale enough during the day. We rush our breathing process, and sometimes we hold our breath. Paying attention to the breath brings an awareness of these habits.

You might notice that your breathing is irregular. Sometimes you might not exhale completely; you inhale a little sooner than is natural. If you don't give in to any tendencies to control your breathing, it will start to relax and regulate itself.

One of my students said that during this exercise she felt the air going into her lungs more deeply, her body felt more relaxed, and her mind became tranquil. This is an accurate description of the process. The mind slows down partly because you're not doing anything; you're taking a break from activity. But usually when you "do nothing," the mind is still filled with a stream of random thoughts. In this case, by consciously directing your attention to the details of breathing, you remove your attention from the stream of random thoughts, and the mind is filled only with the simple process of breathing. You accomplish a minivacation from daily cares.

Because this practice allows us to breathe more easily, it relaxes the body as well as the mind. As more oxygen enters the cells, the whole system breathes more easily and lets go. Sometimes one of my students arrives at a lesson in a particularly distracted state and discovers that something she played well the day before now sounds edgy and rough. After doing this breathing exercise for a couple of minutes, she feels refreshed, and her playing becomes freer and smoother.

To get a feeling for the power of this technique, try singing or playing your instrument for a minute or so without doing the breathing exercise first. Then do the exercise for two minutes and start again. Notice the difference in your state of mind and in the music.

Environment

As your mind slows down and becomes less filled with random thoughts, it becomes more filled with present sensory reality. The texture of the breath, the solidity of your body on the seat, and the air, the light, and the sounds around you enter the foreground of your awareness. It feels good to become more aware of your body instead of living so much in your head. We need this physical aliveness to make music.

After focusing on your breathing for a couple of minutes, you can expand your awareness by deliberately noticing the ground beneath you and the space around you. Notice your body giving in to gravity as you rest solidly on the seat or stand on the floor. The more rooted and balanced you feel, the easier it is to relax and to be aware of the space around you. Notice the expanse of open space between the walls. Let the atmosphere in the room affect you.

This experience is so basic that we usually overlook it. But practicing this kind of awareness prepares us for performance, when awareness of the environment is intense. In performance, the rush of adrenaline flooding the body and the energy coming back to us from the audience overwhelm us and interrupt our usual mental chatter, making the mind "go blank." By practicing letting the mind unwind through mindfulness of breathing, we become accustomed to an open, uncluttered mind, and experiencing it during performance is less of a shock.

Setting the Stage

Once you settle down, you attain sufficient peace of mind to focus on your work. You have set the stage to express yourself. It's like hanging up your friends' coats so you can relax together in your home, or sitting down at a well-set table to enjoy a meal. Relaxing in the environment allows you to approach practicing with the same kind of ease and joy.

Being settled doesn't mean that your energy is flat or that the music will sound boring. On the contrary, it means you are relaxed and alert, and your energy is unfettered and ready to move at your command. Letting yourself breathe enables you to breathe life into the music.

Beginning a performance from such a composed state sets a wonderful tone for the concert. It projects a calm confidence and a receptiveness to the audience. An arrogant performer might rush onto the stage as if to declare "Here I am!" and charge into the music before the audience has even settled into their seats. But a truly confident performer takes her time and welcomes the audience with a warmth you can feel. By practicing with composure, you cultivate confidence for performing; you learn to be comfortable wherever you are, and to accommodate whatever is happening.

So let yourself breathe, and start your practice session with a clear mind. Take a minute to enjoy just being at ease in your surroundings. See what kind of music you make when you feel comfortable and settled in your own body.

QUESTIONS AND ANSWERS

Question: *Why do you keep your eyes open in this technique? Isn't it more relaxing to close your eyes?*
Answer: The point is that you don't have to shut out your environment to relax. You can be relaxed and alert at the same time. You don't have to space out. If you're so tired that your eyes naturally close, that's fine. But then you might be too tired to do good work. Try keeping your eyes open. Just by staying with it, you start to settle down.

Question: *I don't understand the importance of having an awareness of the ground and space. What if you're in a performing situation, with that element of danger, and you notice the ground and space too much? You might get thrown by the whole environment, and that would interfere with your control of the piece.*
Answer: Many performers think that if they notice what's happening, if they notice the audience and where they are, they won't be able to focus on what they're doing. That can happen if you practice in a narrow, self-involved way, unaware of the environment, because you set yourself up for a contrast. Suddenly face-to-face with an audience, you find the

openness of the space impossible to ignore. Musicians frequently have memory lapses when they get distracted by the environment—the energy in the hall, or the sound of someone coughing. They lose focus because they're not used to allowing the environment into their mind.

If you *practice* allowing the environment into your mind, it becomes part of your everyday experience. You get used to having a vivid awareness of the environment, and it ceases to be threatening. It becomes a nurturing, fertile situation in which you can relax and then focus on your activity at the same time. As long as you focus primarily on what you're *doing* in that space, you can afford to feel the energy around you. The breathing exercise helps you begin to recognize how comfortable and free you can be.

Openness to the environment allows more communication with an audience. Some performers protect themselves from the fear of performing by pretending the audience isn't there or by trying to ignore everyone. Instead, you can include them in your performance. They will feel the difference, and the music you make will have more vitality.

Question: *Sometimes I stop during the day and think, "I haven't breathed in hours." My breathing gets so shallow that it feels as though I haven't been breathing. I actually have to stop and watch myself breathe to realize I* have *been breathing all that time, but in a very minimal way. It's scary.*
Answer: It's scary because the breathing you were doing was scared breathing.
Q: *That's it. If you notice your breath is shallow, should you practice deep breathing? Should you try to get rid of this fear by deliberately changing how you breathe, or just acknowledge the fear?*
A: You can just acknowledge it and let it be. That way you give the *fear* room to breathe, and it eventually relaxes. Deep breathing is a different technique, and a few deep breaths can

also be helpful. But I usually don't take deep breaths. If you let your breath be as it is, you might at some point spontaneously take a breath that's very deep. You don't have to force it.

Question: *Noticing my environment makes me wonder what the best time of day is to practice. When are you most receptive to the environment and to practicing?*
Answer: This is a very personal thing. As with any other kind of work, some people do better in the morning while others prefer the afternoon or evening. Generally, the beginning of the day is good for me, because I feel fresh. But sometimes the evening is a great time to practice, if you're not too tired, because you've dealt with the business of the day and it's not on your mind.

The most important thing is not to overpractice but to do high-quality work. I used to waste time when I practiced with a cluttered mind. I spent a lot of time indulging my emotions at the piano instead of settling down and working intelligently.

If you're exhausted or tense, and you know you can't do any productive work, don't try. Taking a few minutes to relax and let your breath go out can help, but sometimes you just need to rest or take care of something else that is demanding your attention.

Question: *Do you also pay attention to your breathing when you're performing? You breathe, obviously, but how much do you need to breathe when you're playing?*
Answer: I'm sure it's different if you're a singer or a wind player, because the breath is essential to producing the sound, but I don't think about breathing when I'm playing. In order to relax *before* performing, I spend time focusing on the breath. That clears my mind and makes me feel more present.

Question: *When I perform, I just focus on the music and that helps me be present. Isn't that enough?*

Answer: It helps, but see what happens if you take a little time to slow down before you start. On the day of a performance, musicians instinctively slow down. They know that if they just rush onto the stage for their debut recital after riding on a train, running to the hall, and barely making it in time, they won't play their best.

What you're describing is great. I wish more performers would immerse themselves in the music and not worry so much about how they're doing. Keep it up.

Question: *This breathing technique seems to be a modified form of meditation. Do you do real meditation before you practice, and do you teach that to students?*

Answer: I practice meditation, but I don't tell my students to meditate. The commitment to regular meditation practice is personal and requires genuine motivation. If a student gets curious and wants to learn to meditate, I help him find a good meditation instructor, but I don't mix meditation instruction with piano lessons. They're two different things.

There are many kinds of meditation. In the kind I practice, you let go of random thoughts and notice what's happening in the present moment. When a meditator sits and pays attention to her breathing, that's what she's doing. The breath is a present-moment reality. Usually the mind goes from one thought to another without a break. Meditation gives your mind a rest from its stream of preoccupations. It allows you to unwind.

CHAPTER 5

Tuning into Your Heart

Step Three: Tune into your heart.

My student Andrea describes playing background music for a wedding reception the day after she had her heart broken by a failed romance. She sat at a concert grand piano playing old-fashioned love songs while the guests sat at tables, eating and engaging in lively conversation. She had played for such events many times, but this time was different because she was so vulnerable. "I couldn't stop feeling sad," she said. "It was like a flood. I just had to feel it and play, and something came through in the music that had never been there before." Soon after she began playing, she noticed that several groups of guests had stopped talking and were listening attentively. Each time she stood up to leave the room for a break, they burst into applause. "They beamed these big smiles at me," she said. "I didn't feel like a background musician at all. I felt like I was giving a real performance."

"It sounds like your heart was open," I told her, "and they heard it. That's what people want when you play. They want to hear your heart."

I was the audience for such a performance when Julie, another student, came to her lesson a few days after her dog died. She felt raw and tender; all her defenses were down. Although she played the same Chopin études she had struggled with for months, she suddenly found the notes falling into place without effort, straight from the heart. Her entire lesson was some of the most stellar music-making I have ever heard.

Do we have to be let down in a romance or go through the death of a loved one in order to make music from the heart? No, but we do need to be in touch with our heart's longing for love, for music, and for life. We need to remember our vulnerability: At any moment we might lose something that brings us happiness, and ultimately, when we die, we must say goodbye to the entire world. Such thoughts pierce the heart, and the initial shock of that piercing is painful. But it releases a flood of buried emotions, leading us to deeper levels of joy and artistic power.

When we practice, the heart is often obscured under multiple layers of mental and emotional preoccupations. We are distracted by countless judgments of ourselves and by random thoughts. We may feel anxious about getting the music ready to meet a deadline. We may resent having to practice, or we may be overly excited about practicing and dive in with insufficient sensitivity. These habitual mental and emotional states keep us from noticing the raw, sweet, unbearably tender feeling we have for music. We don't need these habitual states of mind. We need access to the throbbing heart beneath them.

Summoning your heart's power is the final preparatory step before practicing, *Step Three: Tune into your heart.* Whatever state of mind you're in, this step allows you to penetrate the heart's protective shield and enter the world of intense warmth and vitality.

This breaking open of the heart happens automatically when you are about to perform; you feel your heart beating. You also feel it when a striking event jolts your mind into full consciousness of reality: You're sitting in a coffee shop looking out the window and daydreaming, when suddenly you hear a crash of dishes, some gasps, and someone yelling in panic, "Is there a doctor in the house?" Or you're attending the wedding of a good friend, and as she walks down the aisle to be married you are unexpectedly overwhelmed by your happiness for her and begin to cry.

Recalling such feelings is how to tune into your heart. To begin, try reflecting for a couple of minutes on the opportunity you have to practice. Not everyone has this opportunity, yet we take it for granted. We want to get it over with and get on to the next thing. Or we feel lethargic and find it hard to get started: "Ugh, I have to practice." We need to wake up. We need to remember who we are and what we are doing. We are not just, ugh, practicing. We are connecting to the heart and mind of a great composer, and to the extent that we are able to do that, we connect with and nourish ourselves.

In the documentary film *From Mao to Mozart: Isaac Stern in China,* a Chinese man speaks about how he was imprisoned in a dark cell for fourteen months because he had committed the crime of playing Western music. The movie is filled with both Chinese and Western music, beautifully played. As I watched it, I tried to imagine the depth of this man's suffering in being denied such musical sustenance and in being punished severely for engaging in the life-giving activity of making music. I realized how much we take for granted the opportunity to live with music every day.

When musicians develop injuries that interrupt their practicing for months, they get depressed. Cut off from the communion with great music, they feel deprived of an essential food. We forget so easily our *need* to practice. So stop for a minute and think about the chance you have. You never know when you might lose it. Even if nothing ever interrupts your musical life, sooner or later your life will end. Remembering this fact can inspire you to make the most of the time you have.

Tuning into the heart is especially helpful when you've had a hectic day. Sometimes a student comes into a lesson extremely keyed up and distracted. Even after sitting and watching his breath go out for a while, his playing still sounds jangled and mechanical. I ask him to close his eyes and think about how he would feel if he received a phone call later that day saying a close friend or relative was just killed in an accident. As he sits quietly for a minute or two, his face and body soften. Tension dissolves. When he opens his eyes and plays again, the difference is like night and day. In place of the jangled and mechanical performance is a deeply human and affecting one.

I'm not suggesting that you dwell excessively on morbid, painful topics. Just reflect on the preciousness of life. This may sound extreme, but it's simply being realistic. It's really possible that tomorrow you won't be here. I told this to a student once, and she looked at me as though I were a little crazy. She was eighteen, and it was hard for her to imagine her life being cut short. A few days later she phoned me and said that her seventeen-year-old sister had just died. "Now I understand what you were talking about," she said.

Another student called from Alabama once to cancel his lesson because he was attending his cousin's funeral. "She was only thirty-eight," he said. "She was in a car accident, and she went into a coma and died. It's so shocking. You never think it's going to happen to you, or to anybody you know or care about."

As you are reading this, someone precious to you may have died without your knowing it. Take one or two minutes now to stop and imagine that this is true.

When you reflect on the impermanence of life, you feel the heart area of your chest open up—it feels warm. Once the heart is open, it is available for whatever activity you engage in. The warmth quickly floods your system. Your body feels more relaxed and fluid inside, and your movements become more gentle and precise. The energy of your heart fuels your actions.

Heart Awareness of the Environment

Once you have uncovered your heart energy, you can extend it into the environment. Here you are in an ordinary room, with your instrument, and nothing's happening. But you're not just in this room. You can hear sounds outside; maybe you hear cars on the street or people talking. Whether you're in a city or in the country, you're among a vast variety of human beings and of life of all kinds. You're in a world. Feel that.

Then, look at your book of music. Maybe it costs only six dollars. But it was written by Beethoven, and it's sitting in front of you. Take a minute to feel the power in that; this brilliant, profound, fiery person named Ludwig van Beethoven was alive two hundred years ago, and the music he wrote still moves us today. So the environment contains the possibility of bringing the power and majesty of the past into the vibrant present moment.

When you are practicing for a performance, the situation is even more intense. At a designated time, eight o'clock on Thursday night the twenty-third, at such-and-such hall, people who have bought tickets will come in and sit down in rows, and you will walk in and play . . . *Beethoven.* Contemplating such an event is a little like gazing at a star-filled sky; you can't help but feel humble and human.

As you begin to appreciate your environment, you may feel the desire to rearrange a few things in it to create an atmosphere that is conducive to intelligent practicing. In a spacious, uncluttered room you can easily relax and focus on your work. But if the piano is heaped with books and everything is a mess, you may find your mind feels messy, too, that it's hard to focus on the details of practicing.

Preparing the environment for an activity helps to ready us psychologically for what will take place. When we invite friends into our house or apartment, we usually clean it up first, make room for our guests, and look forward to them arriving and enjoying themselves. Sometimes we imagine them noticing how our home looks and appreciating it as an expression of who we are. By preparing for something personal and intimate to happen, we energize ourselves and become more receptive to our guests.

You can do the same thing for Mozart. You are about to play his music, to bring him to life in this room. Even if you are in a practice room at school, you can put your coat and bag in an appropriate place and put your scores on the music stand in an orderly fashion.

We tend to take practicing casually. We think, "What difference does it make if I play in an offhand way when nobody's listening? So what if the room's full of junk?" But when the moment of performance comes, we wish we'd practiced with more heart. We think, "My God, everything depends on me. All these people have taken the time and trouble to come and hear me. They're paying money." We wouldn't dream of putting a piano onstage heaped with stuff. It would detract from the performance. A simple, elegant practice environment prepares us for the wide open space of performance, where the spotlight is on us and our heart is exposed.

Exposing the heart is frightening. But without a palpable heart, we are neither fully musical nor fully human. The heart is a storehouse of energy that is always available to us. The more we release this energy, the more joy and meaning we discover in music and in life. Feel your heart. Trust it, in all its rawness and unpredictability. This is your power. Let it flood your being.

Questions and Answers

Question: *How does feeling sad prepare you to play happy music?*
Answer: We think of happy and sad as opposites, but they're actually inseparable, like life and death. Joy would be meaningless if we never experienced sorrow, and it is because of the contrast between the two that we get tears in our eyes when we feel extremely happy. True joy always contains an element of sadness, because it comes from a heart that knows the preciousness, the transitory nature, of experience.

You could play Mendelssohn's "Wedding March" like a happy idiot, or you could play it with tears of joy for the man and woman who are embarking on their life journey together. The first way would be nothing special; the second could thrill everyone present.

Question: *I would like to create the spacious kind of environment you describe, but I have an upright piano against the wall, and it never feels spacious. I feel as though I'm facing a dead end, that the sound isn't free to go out and fill the room. Should I put it in the middle of the room?*
Answer: You have to work with the space you have. You could hang a mirror on the wall over the piano at an angle that gives you a view of what's in back of you. You could also move the piano away from the wall a little to create space for the sound to resonate. You might not want to put the piano in the middle of the room because the back of an upright looks like

the underside of a grand piano, with all the beams. But you could cover the back with a nice piece of fabric.

Question: *When I practice, my mind is always bickering with me, saying, "You shouldn't be doing this; you should be doing something else. Other people play better than you. Why are you still trying?" How can I stay with the heart quality of what I'm doing when such negative thoughts enter my mind? Maybe you don't have such thoughts.*

Answer: Everybody has those thoughts. But they're just thoughts. Once, when the conductor Arturo Toscanini and the cellist Gregor Piatigorsky were about to go onstage to perform together, one of them said to the other, "How are you feeling?" "Terrible," he answered, "because I'm no good." "I'm not any good either," the first said, "but we're no worse than the rest of them. Let's go." Realizing that great, famous artists have such doubts can help you relax.

What's dangerous is the person who thinks he's hot stuff and doesn't have any sense of vulnerability. Once he's onstage, he's bound to feel nervous just like everybody else, and if he's not prepared for that it can throw off his concentration.

Some of our thoughts about our ability are realistic. After studying an instrument for many years, you get an idea of how far you can go. But as long as you want to make music, do it, regardless of how you compare with others. Music is yours to enjoy, and you don't have to chastise yourself for not being like someone else. It's what you do with what you have that makes the difference in your life.

The more you feel your heart, the better you will play. When negative thoughts come up during your practicing, just notice them without identifying with them. Your thoughts are not you. They're just thoughts, habits. Your heart is you.

Question: *It sounds fine to appreciate your environment if you're at home listening to the cars riding by, but what if you're in a practice room at school and hearing your competitors practicing in the next room, and you know they're hoping that you fall on your face, that you won't be able to get through a difficult piece?*

Answer: It's sad that so much energy frequently goes into wishing other people ill and desperately holding on to one's own professional territory or potential professional success. It makes life difficult for a young musician who hasn't yet had time to develop a successful career and is bound to have doubts about her ability. If you feel hurt by destructively competitive people, remember that their desire to see you fail comes from their own sense of weakness and inadequacy. A truly confident student does not need to put others down to feel strong herself, or to cheat someone else out of a chance to succeed in order to feel good about her own future.

Seek out friendships with more sensitive students who have the maturity to admit their own feelings of inadequacy and to sympathize with you instead of cutting you down. When you are in your practice room, don't be afraid to feel your vulnerability, and let it pour into the music. You can take pride in your sensitivity and know that the destructive attitude of your colleagues is keeping them from developing the tenderness that music needs. Ultimately, you can even feel sad for them, that they lack the courage to be more human.

CHAPTER 6

Basic Mechanics

Step Four: Use your body in a comfortable and natural way.

In 1983, Joan Campbell Whitacre saw me perform and warned me that my habits of repeatedly leaning forward, swaying around, and dropping my wrists below the keyboard were going to get me into trouble. She had just come back from a performing arts medicine conference where she learned about instrumental techniques that cause injury. I responded to her kind warning with arrogance: "You don't know, because you don't play." Fortunately, a year and a half later, my posture and wrist position changed naturally as I became a more relaxed person. One day I simply found myself sitting upright instead of leaning and swaying as I used to, and although my wrists remained flexible, I no longer let them drop so low.

I was shocked. This simpler physical approach felt natural, and when I tried playing the old way, it felt uncomfortable and forced. I didn't know if I should trust the new way of playing after doing something completely different for my whole life.

I asked a musician friend to listen to me play and tell me how it sounded. After hearing ten minutes of Bach and

Chopin, she delivered the verdict: "It sounds much better than before. You're not holding on to the music for yourself; it's coming through more to the listener. You're communicating more."

I knew she was right. I realized that all the leaning and swaying I used to do was a way of struggling against the music, that instead of letting it flow freely through my body, I had been trying to keep a grip on it, to force it to go a certain way. I no longer felt the need to do that. I could sit and move simply, allowing the music to flood my system and naturally pour out of me. Excited by this discovery, I taught the new, upright posture to my students. Every one of them immediately played more beautifully.

Most musicians are not lucky enough to spontaneously discover a better way of using their bodies. They may suspect something is wrong when practicing becomes an endless battle for control of the instrument. Or they may develop an injury that forces them to look for a new technical approach. But many feel just as I did: They enjoy making music and are unaware that it could feel and sound even better.

Every musician needs a working knowledge of the body mechanics involved in using his or her instrument. Posture and movement have enormous impact on one's ability to control an instrument and on how the music sounds. Regardless of talent, musical imagination, and exhortations from teachers to play with a more velvet or penetrating tone, if the body isn't working efficiently, the music that comes out will be only a fraction of what lives inside the person.

Step Four is to *use your body in a comfortable and natural way.* Completely natural movement in making music requires a developed sensitivity and thorough study extending far beyond the scope of this book. This chapter will present a few basic principles of body mechanics and movement dynamics that can make the difference between a fluent technique and one that is uncomfortable and potentially injurious. Although it will focus particularly on piano technique, I will also describe how these principles apply to other instruments.

In preparing this chapter, I interviewed physicians, physical therapists, and movement educators specializing in the Alexander Technique, Bartenieff Fundamentals, Body-Mind Centering, and Laban Movement Analysis. All of them provided valuable information about physiology, body mechanics, and movement dynamics from their extensive experience with musicians' physical problems. I also spoke to teachers of voice and other instruments who have successfully retrained performers suffering from tension and injuries. If you would like to contact any of these health professionals or music teachers, you will find them listed in the Resources for Musicians section at the back of this book.

Before getting into principles of posture and movement, it may be helpful to discuss a few important factors that affect musicians' bodies.

Mechanics, Habits, and Emotions

Musicians are often unaware of how they use their bodies. When an injured instrumentalist comes to a performing arts clinic for a consultation, a doctor sometimes videotapes her playing to see if her posture and movement habits could have caused the injury. Often, she is shocked by the instrumental technique she sees on the screen: It is awkward, inefficient, and full of tension. One musician said, "I wouldn't let my students play that way," and burst into tears.

A student playing in one of my master classes leaned over the keyboard at a 45-degree angle throughout her performance. When I adjusted her posture upright, she felt more ease in playing. Nevertheless, in two subsequent classes, she leaned over just as before, unaware that she was not sitting up straight. One day I ran into her in the subway. She said she was on her way to Macy's to buy a full-length mirror so she could check her posture at the piano.

Using a mirror is a good idea. Alexander teacher Hope Martin explains that when habits are deeply ingrained we lose awareness of what we're doing. "Our kinesthetic sense—our sense of the body's position and movement—adapts to our habits and reads them as 'right.' So we may think we're sitting or moving one way when we're really doing something quite different." More than once I've sat or stood sideways in front of a mirror, turned my head to check my posture, and discovered that I was leaning backward or arching my back when I thought I was upright.

Body awareness is especially difficult for musicians because of the emotional nature of music. Emotional energy floods the body in music-making and distracts us from mechanics. Imagine being overjoyed or furious with someone while carrying a cup of tea across the room; it's hard to be smooth and coordinated in the heat of strong emotional energy.

Working with the production of musical sound involves pleasure and sometimes pain. When we experience pleasure, hormones are released into the system, making us even more receptive to sensation. So sensation builds, and our feeling capacity keeps expanding. We hear a lush, passionate section in a piece of Chopin and feel a rush of warm energy spreading through the body. The more we hear it the more we want to hear it again, until we feel saturated. It's a love affair.

How we react to all of this sensation is crucial. We typically react to pleasure by trying to hold on to it. The hands, arms, back, and neck contract and grasp as our passion for the music becomes possessive. This contracting and grasping is tense and uncomfortable. We habitually react to such discomfort by tightening even more, sometimes to the point of creating pain.

Resisting these tendencies takes constant practice and is the essence of musical discipline.

Understanding these tendencies can help us slow down and be more aware of how we use our bodies. The issue of emotional habits will be addressed in Chapter 8, but understanding and focusing on simple body mechanics can go a long way to release us from the hold of emotional reactions.

Musicians Are Athletes

Musicians don't usually think of themselves as athletes, but they are. While sports like running and football tax the big muscles of the body, practicing a musical instrument makes extreme demands on small muscles. If a musician's little finger feels a bit strained, he might think it's nothing compared to a runner's sore legs. But it can actually be a more serious problem. Here's why.

Muscles are composed of individual fibers. A small muscle depends on relatively few fibers to accomplish a task. When we use small muscles to make rapid, repetitive movements for hours every day, those few fibers are getting a much harder workout than the slower-moving fibers in a runner's leg muscles. In addition, the muscles at the periphery of the body receive less blood than those closer to the center because the blood vessels are smaller, making small muscles still more vulnerable to injury.

We think we aren't working so hard because our heart and lungs aren't pushed like those of a basketball player. Because the whole body doesn't feel tired, we don't realize when we need a break. So we go for hours on end, pushing those little muscles harder and harder, repeating the same movement patterns countless times, unaware of the strain that's building up.

Muscular Tension and Release

Like the strings of a musical instrument, the body must be neither too tight nor too loose to be in tune for making music. Most of us are too tight. We don't realize that we are using more muscular force than necessary. When the skeleton is properly aligned, it doesn't take much force to make even a very loud sound with an instrument. Teachers who retrain musicians find that excess effort is a common problem. Instrumentalists grip too hard with their hands. Singers tighten the muscles in the neck and torso trying to get a big sound.

Physical therapist and Alexander teacher Deborah Caplan helps musicians release tight muscles. "I define released muscles as muscles that are working efficiently for the task they're performing," Ms. Caplan says. "So if you're lifting five hundred pounds, they're going to be working harder than if you're lifting a feather. But many people lift a feather as though they're lifting five hundred pounds."

Physical therapist James Wang explains that muscles work best from a resting or slightly stretched position. Let's say you are playing a chord on the piano. To make the keys go down, you have to contract muscles in your arm. When you contract a muscle, different types of muscle fibers slide past one another in opposite directions, making the muscle shorter.

If you begin your move to play the chord with a relatively relaxed arm (using just enough muscular effort to hold the arm in position), the fibers in each muscle have a long distance to travel, which gives power to your movement. It's like delivering a punch from a foot away instead of an inch: The longer the distance, the more power you have. But if you initiate the movement with a tight muscle (one that is already quite shortened), the fibers have less sliding room, so your movement has less power. If you imagine tightening up your whole body and then trying to run, it becomes obvious that excess muscular tension prevents smooth, powerful performance.

Dr. Patrick Fazzari points out that we need our muscles not only for power but also for endurance, speed, and control. Tight muscles fatigue more easily and cannot perform at top speed. And even if you are playing or singing a short, slow piece of music, fine motor control is impossible when muscles are tense. Dr. Fazzari compares a body with tight muscles to a car whose engine is revving too much at a stoplight: When the light turns green and you have to move, you are overly ready to go, and your vehicle (or your body) goes out of control. In contrast, a car that is idling properly, or a muscle that is in a resting position, with relaxed, normal tone, will be easy to control when you need to move. You can play pianissimo or execute a difficult leap more easily when your muscles are relaxed.

The importance of muscular relaxation extends beyond the muscles of the playing or singing mechanism. When the body is loose and open inside, it serves as a resonating chamber for the sound produced by the instrument. The music vibrates freely within you because you are not constricted. These unrestricted vibrations in the body travel back into the instrument and create a full, rich sound.

From her experience as a voice teacher, Jeannette Lovetri says, "Everyone's voice is beautiful at the core. There's no such thing as a human voice that's not beautiful." It's a question of loosening up the mechanism and the whole body so that nothing obstructs what is naturally present within the person. Likewise, good coordination and the beautiful instrumental sound that comes from it are natural to the human body. We just have to undo whatever habits are in the way.

Exertion and Recuperation

Health professionals advise maintaining a balance between exertion and recuperation in using the body. In comfortable, healthy movement, we allow enough time for muscles to rest between contractions. We also vary our movement patterns to avoid putting undue stress on any particular muscle group. We do not behave like machines; we listen to how our body feels and give ourselves room to relax.

But the musician who practices the same passage sixty-eight times in a row is not listening to his body's need for change and rest. Excessive repetition of a movement causes muscle fibers to lose their elasticity and become shortened. Physical therapist James Wang believes overused muscles develop "oxygen debts." Every time you contract a muscle it needs to get a new supply of oxygen from the blood. If you contract it too often, it doesn't have enough time to get the oxygen. A body that lacks sufficient oxygen becomes more acidic, which damages tissues. Mr. Wang believes that this damage happens locally in particular parts of muscles, causing them to lose power.

To avoid muscle strain, health professionals recommend taking frequent practice breaks. Take a ten- or fifteen-minute break at least every forty-five minutes. Some doctors recommend breaks every twenty-five or thirty minutes. And if your body feels stiff or tight during a session, stretch for a minute or two before continuing.

We may think sitting or standing in one position doesn't take much effort, but it taxes the muscles that support the body in that position. If you walked for two hours you'd feel basically fine afterward, because you would have used different muscle groups in alternation. But if you tried to stand in one position for two hours without moving, it would be a strain. That's similar to practicing without a break.

Muscles need to change position. We even shift positions when we sleep—about twenty-eight times a night. In fact, if you're so tired that you sleep like a rock, you may wake up feeling stiff because the body was too fatigued to shift position more than a few times during the night. Some muscle groups didn't get enough of a break.

Effects of Childhood Training

Starting to study an instrument at a young age can create unique problems. Dr. Fadi J. Bejjani points out that before the age of ten the skeleton is still malleable and is shaped by how you play your instrument, so children need to learn the right habits from the beginning.

Musicians are also especially vulnerable between the ages of ten and sixteen, when the body grows very fast but its parts are growing at slightly different rates. The bones might grow a little faster than the ligaments or tendons. Children adapt to these changes in awkward ways with their instruments, which can have a harmful effect. Dr. Bejjani feels that during this awkward period musicians set themselves up for most injuries later on. He points out that at this age musicians also start entering competitions and auditioning, which causes them to push themselves and thus create further physical stress. Teachers need to be sensitive to these issues.

Respecting Your Individual Body

Teachers also need to encourage students to capitalize on their physical strong points and to avoid repertoire that does not suit their body. Hand therapist Caryl Johnson points out that in addition to hand size and shape, hand flexibility varies greatly from one person to the next. Some musicians naturally have loose connective tissue in their body. If the ligaments (which connect bones to other bones) and the fascia (which encase the muscles and connect them to other muscles) are particularly loose, it can be hard to maintain a strong hand position.

Ms. Johnson is a pianist herself and has unusually flexible hands, which she finds to be both an advantage and a disadvantage. "I can play four- or five-voice fugues with no problem," she says. "But I'm in trouble with Rachmaninoff or Liszt, in pieces where you need a big reach *and* strength." Many patients come to her with injuries that could have been avoided if they had stuck to repertoire that didn't stress their hands.

In addition to musicians' vulnerability to their teachers, those who play in orchestras are subject to the ideas and attitudes of conductors. It is difficult to notice the needs and signals of your body when an authority figure is instructing you to do things a certain way. Many musicians force their bodies to do whatever is asked of them because of the economic imperatives that go with their profession.

In applying the physiological and movement principles presented in this chapter, I encourage you to pay close attention to how your body feels every step of the way. Do not go faster than you can, and do not force your body to do anything. Your practice time is yours alone. It is a time to let go of pressures and to let your body relax, open up, and make music. If you notice tension or discomfort, stop and let it subside before you continue. If you wish, use the information in this chapter to try to discern what you have done that might have caused the tension. If discomfort recurs or persists, stop practicing, consult a physician, and seek expert advice on your technique.

Principles of Posture and Movement

Performers display a wide variety of physical styles. Glenn Gould and Vladimir Horowitz sat low and crouched over the keyboard; Arthur Rubinstein sat up straight. Some musicians lean forward, others lean back. Some move in all directions, others sit basically still. Some curl their fingers, others play with flat fingers. Is any one way the right way? Or does it all depend on your personality?

Performing arts physicians find that musicians do have individual differences in their bodies that require adaptations in technique. But they also know that basic principles apply to everyone. Bones are bones, and muscles are muscles. They work in a given way. Health professionals agree that some of the most talented musicians would play even better if they used their bodies more naturally. Although some performers can subject their bodies to unhealthy techniques for years without serious consequences, others have more delicate physical responses and become injured in a short time.

Here is a basic introduction to posture and movement for musicians. Many sections have headings indicating that they apply to specific instruments. You may skip information on whatever instruments you wish and read only material that applies to you.

Posture

I attended a symposium on performing arts medicine at which a doctor showed slides illustrating common physical problems of musicians. The first slide was of an old European painting depicting a group of people playing chamber music. The harpsichordist was hunched over the keyboard with elbows akimbo. The string players were similarly contorted, heads strained to the side, spines and arms in extreme curved positions. Their faces looked pained. He then asked us to imagine this picture with the instruments removed. The room broke into laughter.

We are conditioned to think that making music is a license for using our bodies in strange and uncomfortable ways, and for holding these postures for hours, days, and years on end. We don't like to question or change our habits, for fear of losing our artistic powers. But these strenuous postures do not serve the best interests of either ourselves or the music.

Good posture allows the limbs and breathing muscles to be free and flexible. When the torso is stable, it functions like the trunk of a tree: The limbs move freely without interfering with the balance of the whole organism. I used to think that to get power and expressiveness at the piano I had to lean forward. Most musicians share this habit of straining toward their instrument in some way instead of finding a comfortable posture and letting their arms and hands (or vocal mechanism) do the work.

Some instruments require a fair amount of torso movement, but how you move is crucial. In normal upright posture, with the spine naturally aligned, the head balances easily on top of the spine. When you slump forward, or hunch over, you move the head out of its balanced alignment with the spine, and the neck muscles must work much harder to hold up the head. This tension travels down into the shoulders, torso, arms, and hands. It also travels upward into the jaw and the facial muscles. The entire music-making mechanism is compromised. If you need to lean forward, keep the neck in line with the rest of the spine and bend from the hip joints. (Information on nonupright posture in playing specific instruments appears in "Necessary Deviations from Upright Posture" on page 91.)

In an effort to sit or stand up straight, some musicians go to an extreme and arch their backs, throwing their shoulders back. This posture overtightens the lower back, making it an ineffective source of support and putting constant strain on a few muscles. In a more natural spinal alignment, the muscles in the torso don't have to work hard. The bones, together with the connective tissue, take on the load of the body and support you against the force of gravity.

Posture and Freedom of the Arms

In playing an instrument, the arm (including the hand) functions both as a system of levers and as a conduit for visceral energy. It carries the charge of emotions and hormones from you into your instrument. Therefore, for both good leverage and musical expressiveness, this elegant route from torso to fingertip must be free of unnecessary tension. Shoulder, elbow, and wrist must be efficiently positioned and sufficiently loose for energy to flow through freely.

Tension in the neck and shoulders can put pressure on nerves that lead into the hand, creating pain or numbness in the hand or forearm. Health professionals often find that adopting proper posture alleviates such conditions by releasing tension in neck and shoulder muscles.

Because many neck muscles extend down across the shoulders, tensing the neck by slumping forward creates tension in the shoulders. Try slumping forward as you read this and see what happens in your neck and shoulders compared to when you sit upright. Notice that the tension in the neck and shoulders travels into the arm muscles, too.

Dr. Fadi Bejjani describes the chain reaction this way: The head represents about ten percent of your body weight. When the neck is not positioned advantageously to support the head, the shoulders take on the load. Because this load is too much for the shoulders, it gets transferred to the elbows, then to the wrists and hands, thus potentially hampering their fine-movement capabilities.

Musicians sometimes lower their necks and heads to look down at their hands. Since the spine continues through the neck, lowering the neck alters the alignment of the entire spine, which creates tension in the neck and shoulders that travels into the arms. If you need to look down, try moving only your eyes. Or tilt your head forward from the top of your neck (at the level of your ears) instead of dropping your neck. This way, your spine can maintain a natural, comfortable alignment.

Some pianists who wear bifocals tilt their head backward to see the score while playing. This position also strains the neck and the playing mechanism. If you wear bifocals, consider buying another pair of glasses to meet the requirements of playing your instrument.

Many musicians habitually round their shoulders and hunch over when playing, which limits the movement of the collarbone and shoulder blade. These bones work together with the arm bones whenever you move your upper arm[1] (see Figure 15). The two collarbones and two shoulder blades form a yokelike structure, called the "shoulder girdle," which is suspended over the upper rib cage with muscle and other soft tissue in between. Hunching over throws the shoulder girdle forward and compresses the space between it and the ribs in front, limiting the mobility of the shoulder girdle and arms.

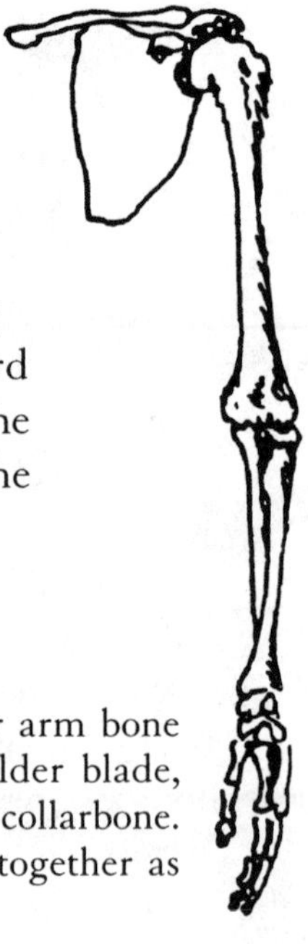

Figure 15 The upper arm bone attaches to the shoulder blade, which attaches to the collarbone. All the bones move together as one mechanism.

The collarbone moves from its joint with the breastbone. Try sitting upright and putting your left hand on your right collarbone. Move your right arm forward and notice that the collarbone moves easily with it. Now hunch over and do the same thing. Notice that the collarbone can hardly move.

Although the shoulder blade attaches to both the collarbone and the upper arm bone, it does not attach to the ribs in back. Instead, it floats in muscle and glides over your back. It is therefore free to move along with the collarbone and provides great mobility of the arm.

When I was giving my first seminars on the Art of Practicing, a few nonpianists asked me to help them with their playing. Although I believe strongly that without mastery of an instrument it is impossible to teach it properly, I agreed to work with a few of these instrumentalists as an experiment. One of them was a cellist who constantly hunched over the cello while playing. I asked him to lengthen the endpin so that he could play in a more upright position much of the time. Immediately his arms moved with more freedom and power, and a bigger, more voluptuous sound came out of the cello.

When the shoulder blade has full range of motion, the freedom affects even the fingers. Joan Campbell Whitacre finds that when a musician begins to move his shoulder blade more freely, he becomes more aware of the connection between the shoulder blade and the fingertips. This feeling of freedom and connectivity results in greater freedom and precision in using the hand. Without a free shoulder blade, the hand and forearm have to compromise their natural position and/or movement to perform on the instrument.

To feel how mobile the shoulder blade can be, sit or stand comfortably upright, reach in back of you with your left hand, and touch your right shoulder blade while moving your right arm forward, back, and to the side. Then try to feel this mobility without actually touching the shoulder blade. Finally, play a few notes on your instrument and feel the connection between the shoulder blade and the tip of each finger. Slowly play part of a piece of music, maintaining this feeling of connectedness. Notice how this connectedness affects your playing.

Musicians often fail to take advantage of the mobility of the shoulder blade. Often when I ask a student to move her arm forward, she moves her torso forward at the same time, as if the two body parts were glued together. Using torso muscles to help push keys down is inefficient. These muscles are big, and moving them is a great deal of work. It's much easier to let the arm move freely while keeping the torso in one place, or letting the torso move slightly backward in reaction to the forward movement of the arm.

Many instrumentalists, such as violinists, wind players, and percussionists, exhibit another common habit that restricts arm movement: They raise their rib cage along with their arms while lifting and playing their instruments. Alexander teacher and percussionist Melanie Nevis says this habit is usually carried over from the activities of daily living. "If you do it when you reach up to the shelf for your dishes, you'll probably do it when you lift your instrument." Moving this way causes the back to arch, creating strain. Moving the arms independently from the torso allows the spine to maintain a more natural and comfortable alignment.

If, instead of raising the rib cage, you collapse the upper torso slightly (a mild version of slumping), you limit breathing in the upper portion of the lungs, which extend upward to the level of the shoulders and outward to the sides of the body. This restriction of movement within the uppermost part of the torso limits the freedom of the shoulders and arms. Joan Campbell Whitacre helped one conductor release tension in her shoulders by teaching her to stand in a way that allowed her upper lungs to move more freely. As a result, "her arms were freer and she could express more freely with the baton."

Freedom and power of the arm in upright posture have a great deal to do with the stability of the body. Sit or stand upright and move your arm straight forward, as if punching something. Then lean forward and punch again. The punch has less power when you give up your solid base of support.

For pianists, leaning forward, whether you slump or not, cramps arm movement, which limits arm flexibility and power (see Figures 16 and 17). In later sections I will describe specific piano techniques that provide maximum power without sacrificing the ease of a comfortably upright torso.

Posture, Circulation, and the Viscera

Collapsing the spine in any way, whether you simply round your shoulders forward or crouch over your instrument, constricts the chest. When the chest is naturally uplifted, the heart and lungs have more room to operate. The resulting free circulation of blood and oxygen nourishes the body, improving function. Beyond this purely functional level, keeping the soft, vulnerable front of the torso uncramped and open allows emotional energy to flow more freely through the viscera. The vital energy of the heart, organs, and glands is more available for making music.

A young woman played in one of my workshops with her shoulders rounded slightly forward. When I had her adjust her upper back to a full upright position, tears filled her eyes and she protested in a child's voice, "I don't like it! It makes me mad! I want to protect myself!" I was impressed with her self-awareness. She understood that she needed to let her shoulders be free, but it made her feel painfully exposed because it opened her up emotionally. In spite of her resistance, she courageously released the tension in her shoulders and played in a more uplifted posture. Her playing immediately

Figure 16 The author demonstrates an inefficient posture for playing the piano: Slumping forward cramps arm movement and creates tension in the neck, shoulders, and arms.

Figure 17 In upright posture, the arms can move freely and the head balances easily on top of the spine, easing the load on the neck, shoulders, and arms.

sounded warmer and richer. The new position gave both her emotions and her arms free range.

Upright posture is part of being human. Animals walk on four legs, and their soft, vulnerable "front" faces the ground. But we face one another fully and exchange emotional energy that way. Laban movement analyst Martha Eddy points out that when we sit or stand in an uplifted way, our organs expand. This fullness, which increases when musical vibrations enter the body, not only lends vital energy to the music but also provides support for the torso, easing the load on the muscles.

Notice how you feel standing or walking in a comfortably uplifted posture versus leaning forward or backward, or hunching over. The feeling your posture creates comes through in the music you make.

Posture, Breathing, and the Throat

For singers and wind players, lung power is crucial, and the torso must be uncompressed and ready to expand. Good posture allows free movement of all the breathing muscles, including the diaphragm, the thoracic muscles, and all the abdominals. Collapsing the spine and chest constricts these muscles. Arching the back also makes breathing difficult by constricting the back muscles. Both a collapsed and an arched posture also put strain on the neck, further restricting air flow (see Figures 18 and 19).

According to trumpeter Stephen Burns, good posture is the key to having an "open throat"—a crucial aspect of brass technique. He points out that rounding the shoulders forward produces tension in the neck, which strains the throat and tongue. Tightening the pectoral muscles also causes neck tension. Some players lift their chin in an effort to free the throat (see Figure 19). This habit causes overstretching of the neck

Figure 18 (left) Trumpeter Stephen Burns illustrates two common problems with posture: Keeping the feet too close together provides insufficient support for the upper body, and collapsing the chest constricts breathing.

Figure 19 Arching the back and lifting the chin constrict air flow and cause strain in the throat and torso.

muscles and, in long-necked players, can even cause the inner lining of the neck (the throat itself) to protrude through these muscles, causing pain. Because the base of the tongue is in the throat, neck tension also interferes with tongue movement, making articulation labored.

Figure 20 Standing with the feet shoulder width apart creates a solid base of support for the torso. Upright posture, with the knees unlocked, allows the lungs and the breathing muscles to move freely.

When wind players stand to play their instruments, bending their knees and pushing their feet into the floor transfers body weight to the floor and simultaneously stimulates a flow of energy upward through the legs and into the lower torso. This movement engages the lower torso and limbs in weight support and transfer, and it releases unnecessary tension in that area, making it more available for generating power through breathing.

If you sit while playing a wind instrument, you can effect a similar release of energy in the following manner: First, establish your posture by placing your feet shoulder width apart and balancing your weight solidly on your feet and your sit bones—the two bones at the base of the pelvis that are designed for balancing easily in sitting posture (see Figure 21). When you inhale, relax your entire torso, allowing the diaphragm to move naturally and the lungs to displace the muscles and organs of the lower torso. Let the rib cage expand and rise. When you exhale, let this process reverse naturally. Keep your postural alignment and allow the abdominal muscles to move fluidly and the rib cage to float so that the chest does not collapse.

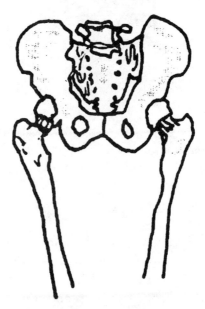

Figure 21 The two sit bones protrude at the base of the pelvis, which attaches to the leg bones at the hip joints.

Some wind players cross their legs while playing seated, which compresses one side of the torso in the hip region and prevents the weight of that side of the torso from resting solidly on the sit bone. As a result, the breathing muscles become engaged in keeping the torso upright and are, therefore, not fully available for the movements of breathing. This posture also locks the hip joints, further preventing natural torso movement and energy flow.

Some singers stand on their toes to sing high notes. Voice teacher James Carson advises against this practice because it creates tension in the leg muscles and the abdominal, intercostal, and chest muscles. This tension continues up into the throat, the palate, and the head, preventing proper control of the breath, which leaves the singer with only one choice: forced breath pressure. It also restricts the muscles that tune the pitch mechanism and inhibits the movements of the speech muscles in the tongue and palate. To avoid these problems, Mr. Carson recommends keeping both feet flat and solid on the floor.

Finding a Good Posture

To find a good sitting posture, balance upright on your sit bones (see Figure 21). You can feel them when you shift your weight on your seat from side to side. Alexander teacher Hope Martin suggests thinking of the sit bones as "feet that support your torso." This image may help you settle firmly and comfortably into your seat. From that solid base, let the spine lengthen upward naturally. Let your shoulders extend out to the sides.

Allowing your neck and jaw muscles to release will help your head find its natural balance on top of the spine and will help the entire spine align itself properly. Feel how your skeleton rocks gently back and forth resting easily on the sit bones. Mentally scan your body from head to toe, releasing any tension you notice in the muscles. Feel a three-dimensional expansion from the center of your torso out, letting yourself breathe fully.

Keeping both feet solidly on the floor gives essential support to the back. Pianists sometimes keep their left heel off the floor, which makes it impossible to maintain an even pelvis, requiring torso muscles to work too hard. Guitarists who use footstools often create a similar imbalance. Guitar teacher

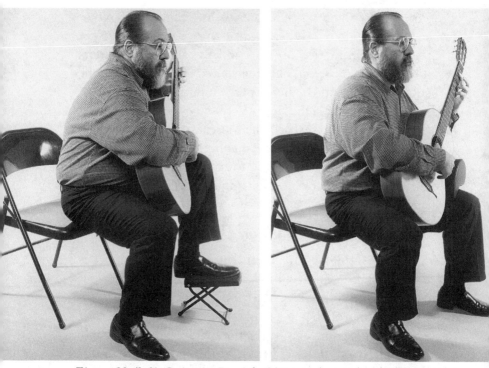

Figure 22 (left) Guitarist Patrick O'Brien shows that bending over to reach the guitar cramps the upper torso and arms. Using a footstool to bring the guitar more within playing range throws the pelvis off balance, which strains the lower back.

Figure 23 Propping up the guitar with a specially designed cushion allows the player to sit naturally upright and to use the arms with ease. Eliminating the footstool and keeping both feet solidly on the floor straightens out the pelvis and provides support for the back.

Patrick O'Brien explains that if a guitarist is short, he can use a footstool without distorting his pelvis very much, but a tall player creates more problems by using a footstool because he has to bend farther over the instrument. Mr. O'Brien says that propping up the guitar with a specially designed cushion, or with an adjustable device called an "A Frame," allows guitarists "to straighten out their pelvis for the first time in centuries" (see Figures 22 and 23).

If you stand to play your instrument, or if you sing, go through the same process, starting with both feet planted solidly on the floor as your base of support. Feel how your entire body balances over your feet. Gravity keeps you rooted, and leg and torso bones and muscles easily hold you up.

Dynamic Balancing

Posture is dynamic, not static. Because we're alive, subtle movements, such as breathing, constantly occur even when we're "sitting still." So it's counterproductive to try to hold a rigid posture. Instead, we need to stay supple in order to respond easily to what the music and instrument require at every moment.

If you play your instrument in a seated position, your weight shifts slightly on your sit bones all the time as you breathe and move your arms. If you play in a standing position, it shifts on your feet. With some instruments, such as the violin, it's natural to shift your weight from one foot to the other as you play, particularly to balance certain arm movements.

Violinists and violists sometimes place their left foot slightly in front of the right, so that when they want to stress notes with the bow, they can lean toward the fiddle and their left foot will be properly positioned to receive their body weight. Keeping the knees unlocked allows the body to move when the music requires it and also allows energy to flow freely through the legs and into the torso.

Body weight also shifts in reaction to movement of an instrument. When a violinist's bow hits a string, the violin moves in reaction. Violinist Frances Magnes advises players to let their body follow the movement of the instrument rather than holding themselves rigidly in place. If you try to prevent the fiddle from moving, your body becomes tense and the instrument becomes "a frozen piece of wood," she says. "The wood has to be alive. It has to move in accordance with the phrasing and other aspects of the music." When you let energy circulate freely back and forth between your body and the instrument, you make more music.

Sit bones and feet are curved structures. Let yourself rest on them by balancing dynamically, not by trying to hold yourself statically in position. You'll rest much easier that way.

Balancing an Instrument

Holding an instrument affects your posture, and posture affects how you hold and play your instrument. Physical therapist and Alexander teacher Deborah Caplan advises instrumentalists to first sit or stand in a neutral, efficient alignment without holding the instrument, and then "bring the instrument to you, rather than compromise the efficiency of balancing the different components of the body in order to go to the instrument." Then, as you move into position for holding the instrument, allow this movement to occur as comfortably and efficiently as possible.

Violin, Viola, and Large Wind Instruments

Ms. Caplan points out that when you are standing and holding an instrument like a violin or a trumpet, having the weight of the instrument in front of the body requires you to lean backward in some way to compensate and to maintain balance. Many players arch their backs to achieve this compensation. Ms. Caplan advises leaning back from the ankles, which doesn't require leaning as far as leaning from the waist and does not distort the alignment of the spine, the rib cage, or the shoulders.

Violist Karen Ritscher finds that arching the back overtightens the lower back, making it unavailable as a source of support for the instrument. She feels that the entire body, including the legs and the pelvis, should provide support for the instrument. Ms. Ritscher recommends using the collarbone and the chest rather than the left shoulder to hold the viola, which frees that shoulder and arm to move easily and makes it unnecessary to strain the neck to the side. In order for the chest to support the instrument in this way, you need to maintain an uplifted posture (see Figures 24 and 25). Ms. Ritscher points out that a violinist can "get away with" using the shoulder to support the violin, but the viola is too heavy.

Because this posture allows the head to face forward, the player can read the score more easily. Ms. Ritscher says that many players habitually keep their eyes on the fingerboard and resist facing forward, but that with the exception of occasional glances at the fingerboard to observe a specific long shift, the eyes and head can be directed forward with no loss of accuracy in playing.

Many violin and viola players tighten the muscles in the neck and squeeze the instrument between the chin and the collarbone to hold it in place. But by relying instead on the weight of the head to keep the instrument in playing position, you eliminate unnecessary strain on the neck and shoulders. Simply release the neck muscles and let the head drop freely onto the instrument.[2]

Frances Magnes finds that many violinists don't hold their instrument high enough. She recommends holding it with the

Figure 24 Violist Karen Ritscher shows how violists and violinists often rely on the chin and the left shoulder to hold the instrument in place. The neck must twist to the side, creating strain in the neck, shoulders, and arms.

Figure 25 By using the collarbone to help support the viola, the player frees the neck, shoulders, and arms from unnecessary strain.

scroll at mouth level. "I find it plays easier that way. If it's lower, you're fighting gravity all the time." Since the viola is heavier than the violin, however, a lower position is more comfortable.

Stephen Burns recommends a "pyramid" type of posture for trumpeters: the feet shoulder width apart, providing a wide, solid base of support, and the legs leading up at opposing angles toward the head. If the feet are too close together, the lateral sense of balance is thrown off because the foundation is too small to support playing the instrument (see Figures 18, 19, and 20).

Flute

According to flutist Janet Weiss, good posture prevents a flute player from placing too much weight on the parts of the body that support the instrument. If you collapse the chest while playing, the flute moves down, away from the support of the chin, requiring the left index finger, right thumb, and right little finger to work too hard to hold it up. This tension in the hand makes playing difficult. Collapsing the chest also creates a disadvantageous angle for the embouchure. Changing to an uncompressed posture corrects these problems (see Figures 26 and 27).

Ms. Weiss adds that the flute never stays in one position all the time. The balance constantly shifts from one support point to another.

Necessary Deviations from Upright Posture

Some instruments require occasional deviations from upright posture to reach extreme hand positions. To play at the very top or bottom of the piano keyboard, for example, you may have to lean to the side, depending on the length of your arms and the hand position and movement required. To reach

Figure 26 (left) Flutist Janet Weiss demonstrates inefficient posture for orchestral playing: Hunching over to see the music and the conductor makes breathing difficult and creates a disadvantageous angle for the embouchure. It also causes the weight of the instrument to fall too heavily on the fingers that support it, creating tension in the hands.

Figure 27 Bending forward from the hip joints allows the spine to remain straight, which gives the lungs more room to function. It also allows the player to hold the flute more easily and use a more comfortable embouchure.

notes at the extreme end of the fingerboard on the guitar or cello, your spine has to move and curve beyond its neutral, upright position. In all such cases, breathe fully to avoid compressing your torso. Instead of hunching or straining, maintain a feeling of length along your entire spine while you move your back, and keep a sense of width across your shoulders while you reach with your arms. At the piano, rotating your torso to the side allows you to reach distant keys without leaning too far.

Percussionists often have to lean forward to reach distant instruments. Melanie Nevis, who is both a percussionist and a

Figure 28 Percussionist and Alexander teacher Melanie Nevis demonstrates awkward posture for reaching distant instruments: Rounding the back and the shoulders strains them and cramps arm movement.

Figure 29 Keeping the torso lengthened while reaching for distant instruments eases the load on the shoulders and allows the arms to move with freedom and power.

teacher of the Alexander Technique, advises keeping the torso lengthened and bending from the hip joints rather than hunching over and collapsing the shoulders. If you are standing, letting your knees bend slightly will help you bend more easily from the hip joints (see Figures 28 and 29).

Orchestral flute players have to lean forward to see the score, to see the conductor, and to avoid hitting the person next to them with the flute. Janet Weiss recommends that instead of hunching over and collapsing the chest, as many players do, players should keep their torso lengthened and bend from the hip joints, so that their breathing isn't constricted (see Figures 26 and 27).

Getting Help with Your Posture

Because it is difficult to feel exactly how we are sitting or standing, it is helpful to receive guidance on your posture from a movement educator. A practitioner of the Alexander Technique, Body-Mind Centering, the Feldenkrais Method, or Laban Movement Analysis can help you align your spine and use your muscles to achieve easy balance and support. Ask him or her to watch you play or sing and to tell you if a different way of supporting and balancing your weight will allow you to move more freely and naturally.

Using the Hands and Arms

Grasping

One of the first things a baby does after it's born is make grasping movements with its hands, wrapping its fingers readily around whatever adult finger is offered. Parents are often surprised at the power of that tiny hand reaching out to hold on to life and other living creatures. The instinct to grasp is so deep that we don't usually stop to question the ways we use our hands or how much they mean to us. We take their power for granted until something reminds us how precious they are.

I remember cutting my little finger badly on the lid of a tin can in the kitchen. Seeing the blood gush out from under a thick flap of flesh, I envisioned the end of my entire musical career and screamed at the top of my lungs, "My finger!" Luckily, no serious damage had been done, and a few stitches patched up my precious finger.

We work hard with our hands, and they bring us great rewards. We maximize these rewards if we use our hands with gentleness. Grabbing an instrument with too much force strains the hands and arms and decreases sensitivity. But yielding to our tender nature and using a minimum of grasping power allows the hands and arms to relax so they can contain more feeling. We discover a truer intimacy with the instrument and the music.

When I was fourteen I began studying with a wonderful teacher in Berkeley named Alexander Libermann. He had a very commonsense way of explaining things. One of the first things he had me do was pick up a pencil and notice the movement my hand made. He pointed out that I automatically knew exactly how much pressure it took to hold the pencil without either squeezing it or dropping it. He explained that playing the piano was the same. Instead of hitting the key, you "take" it, like taking a pencil in your hand. He taught me to use just enough strength to push down the key, and nothing extra.

This kind of awareness is essential in playing all instruments. Excess tension in any of the playing muscles prevents vital energy from flowing freely from the body into the instrument. The details of achieving freedom in your playing mechanism require the personal attention of a qualified teacher. The next sections will present a few basic principles for moving the hands and arms with minimum effort.

Minimum Hand Tension

Health professionals talk about "the position of function" of the hand—a neutral position from which the fingers function with the greatest strength and efficiency (see Figure 30). Dr. Emil Pascarelli suggests finding this position by extending your forearm, not bending your wrist in any particular direction, and turning your hand palm up. The natural curve your hand assumes is the position of function. If you keep that curve and simply turn your hand over onto a piano keyboard, you have a strong, comfortable, loose hand. Whatever instrument you play, staying as close to this model as possible will help you avoid straining your hand and arm. Deviating from

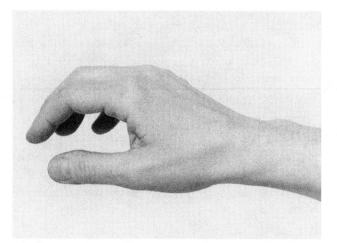

Figure 30 In the position of function the hand forms a natural arch.

it excessively by keeping your fingers raised, curled, or unnecessarily far apart will cause strain.

Instrumental teachers find that students usually play with too much tension in their fingers. Some musicians overexert their fingers to exercise their muscles and strengthen them. The fingers themselves don't have any muscles in them; the muscles that control the fingers are in the rest of the hand and mainly in the forearm. Tendons extend from these muscles to move the fingers. So overtensing the fingers creates excess tension in the forearm. This tension prevents the free flow of energy into the hand, making playing difficult and creating an unpleasant sound.

Piano

Minimum hand tension in playing the piano begins with sitting at the proper height. If your elbow is lower than the top of the white keys, your hand and forearm must reach up to the keyboard, which places the fingers at a disadvantageous angle for pushing down keys and requires the hand to work too hard. Sitting too low also prevents the weight of the arm from dropping directly into the keys to produce sound. The hand and forearm must overwork to compensate.

To prevent such strain, adjust the height of the bench by following these steps:

1. Sit upright on the bench and drop your arms at your sides.
2. Place your hands on the keyboard in position to play with your forearms perpendicular to the length of the keyboard.
3. Let your elbows drop naturally rather than holding them against your body or sticking them out to the side.
4. Raise each wrist to the level of the arch of your hand (see Figure 31).

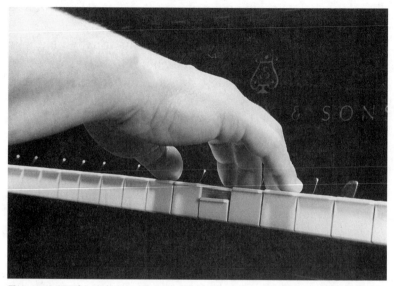

Figure 31 When the wrist is level with the arch of the hand, the fingers need to bend only slightly to depress the keys. This position also allows the weight of the arm to drop directly into the keys, assisting the fingers in producing sound.

5. If your elbows are not level with the white keys, adjust the piano bench until they are. Use a yardstick or metal tape measure to check that the distance between the floor and your elbow is the same as the distance between the floor and the top of the white keys.

While playing, avoid dropping your wrists below keyboard level.

To train your fingers to move with minimum effort, place one hand on the keyboard, keeping the wrist level with the arch of the hand. Practice playing one note at a time with a loose finger while keeping the other fingers relaxed and resting on the keys. Don't use arm movement at first; simply bend the finger to push the key down without trying to get a big sound. Bending primarily from the base and middle knuckles, rather than the tip joint, will allow you to maintain a strong, comfortable, arched position. When you move your index finger to play, the other four fingers should rest on the keys without tension instead of hovering over the keys or sticking up in the air (see Figures 32 and 33).

Slowly play five white keys in succession, starting with the thumb. When each key is down, check to make sure that your other fingers are relaxed and resting on the keys before you play the next note. If one finger is up even a millimeter, the lifting muscles (extensors), which are on the topside of the forearm (the side in line with the back of the hand), are contracting to hold it up. Since you are simultaneously contracting the bending muscles (flexors), which are on the underside of the forearm (the side in line with the palm of the hand), to press a key down, your entire forearm becomes unnecessarily tight. This phenomenon of "co-contraction" creates a harsh tone and limits speed and expressiveness.

To keep the playing finger as loose as possible, visualize the bones of your finger moving instead of focusing on muscle power. Think of the joints as openings where movement takes place, and visualize the lubricating fluid in the joints flowing. Bend each finger loosely toward the palm of your hand.

The thumb works differently than the other fingers. If you move it toward the palm, it goes under the other fingers. We need this movement as well to play the piano; a simple legato scale, for instance, requires passing the thumb under the other fingers every few notes. But to push a key down, the thumb must move vertically instead of bending from the knuckle.

If you learn to use the fingers this way without adding any extra push from the arm, you will have the first foundation of efficient, comfortable movement and a beautiful tone. Even if some fingers are at first too weak to produce sound,

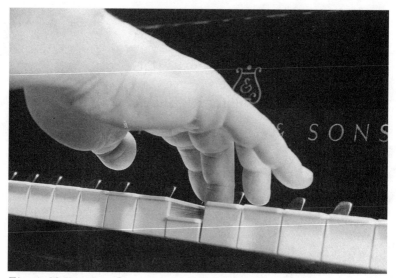

Figure 32 Keeping fingers raised above the keys while other fingers are playing requires unnecessary effort from the muscles in the forearm. The excess tension spreads throughout the hand, inhibiting speed and expressiveness.

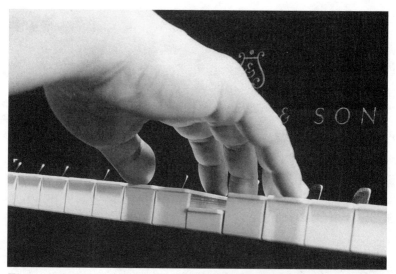

Figure 33 Letting fingers rest on the keys when they are not playing minimizes tension in the hand and forearm, which increases ease and improves tone quality.

keep using them in this relaxed way until they acquire enough strength to make sound. Once this control of your fingers becomes a habit, your mind will be free to focus on adding arm movements to your technique. These will be discussed later.

When playing with relaxed fingers becomes a habit and you have developed wrist and arm freedom as well, you can add a little bit of pressure with the fingerpads (the cushiony part of the fingertips) to produce a penetrating sound. Don't let the hand become tense; just slightly squeeze the key with the fingerpad and keep the hand as loose as possible.

Keeping the hand loose also requires not keeping the fingers spread apart longer than necessary. Opening the hand is more strenuous than leaving it in a neutral position. Choose fingerings that minimize the amount of time your hand is stretched. Also, when reaching a distant key requires you to open your hand, release the stretch immediately after playing that note. So, on the keyboard, if you stretch from your right thumb on middle C to your little finger on the C above, let your other fingers move back to a less open position as soon as you've played the higher note. It's like opening and closing a fan: Open your hand to a full reach, then release the reach to allow the muscles to recuperate. Adding wrist and arm movement, which I will describe later, will make it easier to reach distant keys.

Guitar

Guitarist Patrick O'Brien says that at least nine out of ten injured guitarists who come to him for retraining play with too much tension at the tips of their fingers. He recommends minimizing the use of the tip joints and bending the fingers mostly from the other joints. The reason for this correction is to avoid co-contraction of the flexor and extensor muscles in the arm. While most finger movements use either the flexors (on the underside of the forearm) or the extensors (on the top-side of the forearm), bending from the tip joints makes the muscles on both sides of the arm contract simultaneously.

You can feel this for yourself by experimenting. Place your left hand lightly around your right forearm. Loosely bend one of the fingers of your right hand without bending the tip joint. Notice how your right arm feels. Now bend the same finger mostly from the tip joint. Notice the difference in your arm.

In addition, bending from the tip of a finger makes other fingers move inadvertently. This means you are creating further tension in your arm. Those fingers are then less ready for what they have to do next, because they are busy doing something else.

Mr. O'Brien also points out that when you strike a string using the tip joint, you leave the string on a tiny point in the center of the fingernail, which results in a sharp, thin tone. If you use a longer portion of your finger to play, the last part of the nail to leave the surface of the string is a broad surface, which makes a mellower sound.

Mr. O'Brien explains, "If a string moves back and forth parallel to the frets, it doesn't make much sound. But if the string is pushed down before plucking so that it pops up and moves perpendicular to the frets, it makes a resonant sound. Relaxing the tips of the fingers allows the playing fingers to press the strings down toward the face of the guitar, which results in a full sound. But hooking the tips of the fingers pushes the strings to the side, so that they vibrate parallel to the face of the instrument, resulting in a small sound." Figures 34 through 37 show the contrast between these two ways of plucking a string.

The use of the left hand in playing the guitar is guided by similar principles. Many players tense the shoulder and pull the hand far behind the neck of the guitar. If you use this position, the fingers at rest are already on the strings, in-

Figure 34 Bending a finger from the tip joint to pluck a guitar string creates excessive tension in the forearm muscles that control that joint.

Figure 35 Bending primarily from the other joints eliminates that extra tension.

Figure 36 In addition to creating excessive tension in the forearm muscles, bending the thumb from its tip joint also pulls the string parallel to the face of the instrument, which creates a thin, metallic sound.

Figure 37 Relaxing the tip of the thumb relaxes the muscular co-contraction in the wrist and forearm and presses the string down toward the face of the instrument, creating a fuller, richer sound.

stead of poised above them, so that to release a string you have to lift the fingers instead of just relaxing them. The lifting often creates co-contraction in the left arm: You are simultaneously lifting some fingers (using extensor muscles) while bending others (using flexor muscles). To avoid co-contraction, Mr. O'Brien recommends relaxing the left shoulder and poising the hand over the strings so that the natural lengths of the fingers fall over the strings rather than straining. To make a string go down, flex your finger from the knuckle that connects it to the rest of the hand. To release it, simply relax your finger.

Viola

Violist Karen Ritscher applies similar ideas to using the left hand on her instrument. She suggests finding a position that allows the fingers to "just drop out of the knuckle" instead of straining. Ms. Ritscher says that while players are generally taught to find a hand position by placing their index finger on the fingerboard first and then stretching their other fingers toward the strings, most people need to start with the little finger and work backward. If you let the little finger find a natural, comfortable position first, it won't have to stretch too far. Since many people, particularly women, have especially short little fingers in proportion to the rest of the hand, adopting this position helps keep the hand free of unnecessary tension. Figures 38 and 39 show the contrast between these two positions.

Ms. Ritscher also points out that string players typically press too hard with the fingers of both hands. It doesn't take much force to put down the strings or to hold the bow. If the fingers of the left hand are too tight they lose sensitivity, which makes it impossible to find exact placements for playing in tune. She trains violists to become sensitive to just how much pressure is necessary with each hand, and not to let one hand influence the other. Notice if your left hand presses harder

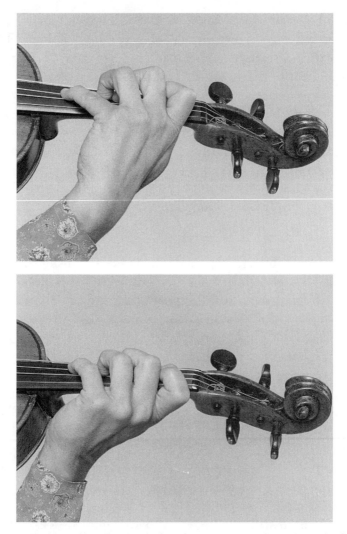

Figure 38 (top) Placing the index finger on the fingerboard of the viola first and then stretching the other fingers into position strains many players' left hands.
Figure 39 Letting the little finger find a comfortable position first and then placing the other fingers on the strings is more natural for many women and other players whose little fingers are particularly short.

than necessary in reaction to bowing forte with the right hand; simple awareness can correct this habit.

As with other held instruments, avoid clutching with the thumb. Relax your grip on the instrument and learn how little force it takes to hold on to it.

Flute

Janet Weiss is another expert on how to play with a loose hand. She discovered years ago that the traditional flute didn't fit her hand, and she became a pioneer in redesigning the instrument to make certain keys easier to reach. "They make instruments like socks," she says. "One size fits all." In researching the history of the flute, she found that there is no musical reason for the instrument to be exactly as it is. Since then, she has helped many other players make their flutes more user-friendly, tailoring them to their individual hands.

Ms. Weiss had one of her keys moved an eighth of an inch down from its original position, and she put a one-millimeter lift on top of the key. She added a quarter-inch extension to another key so that her little finger could reach it easily. She also had her thumb key redesigned for better leverage. Without these adjustments, her hand was constantly strained. "The instrument we're playing is incorrect for many people," she says. "It's like trying to dance in a pair of shoes that don't fit." Flutists with small hands need to change their instrument more than those with bigger hands. Figures 40 and 41 show how Ms. Weiss' modified flute eliminates the need to strain her hand.

After redesigning a student's flute, Ms. Weiss diagnoses where his playing position is faulty. As mentioned earlier, improving posture frees the hands from having to work too hard to support the instrument. "You can't wiggle a finger and bear weight on it at the same time," she points out, "yet people try to do it all the time."

Figure 40 Reaching some of the keys on the standard flute strains many players' hands.

Figure 41 By altering keys with tailor-made lifts and extensions, the flutist can play her instrument without straining her hands.

As a student's playing improves, Ms. Weiss has him practice long tones with relaxed fingers. She finds that most flutists squeeze the keybed instead of pressing with a loose hand. Because teachers have traditionally emphasized the importance of practicing long tones, students tend to play them with a lot of stress. She can tell if a flutist has been tensing his fingers too much if his fingers are stiff after playing a long tone. When the fingers are loose, he's improving.

Other Woodwind Instruments

Ms. Weiss says that many other woodwind instruments are not user-friendly for all players, and that an increasing number of woodwind players are modifying the keys on their instruments to fit their hands. Some clarinetists also use neck straps to hold their instruments in order to take weight off of the right hand and avoid straining it.

Ms. Weiss favors the American style of holding the clarinet vertically over the British style of pointing the instrument somewhat forward. When the horn extends out in front of the player, his right thumb has the burden of supporting the instrument against gravity. But when the bell of the clarinet is pointed down, the thumb is partially relieved of this burden, thus freeing the hand of unnecessary tension. If the edge of the bell rests on the knee, the hand has even less work to do to support the instrument. Ms. Weiss adds, however, that each player has a unique body and must find the angle that works best for him or her. For some, a vertical position may feel extreme, and a slightly slanted one may work best.

Players of reed instruments frequently overtense their hands in making reeds, and this tension carries over into how they play their instruments. Using a reed-making tool with a longer and wider handle can relieve some of the hand strain these players experience.

Trumpet

Trumpeter Stephen Burns says that many players use a "death grip"—they grip the trumpet too hard with one or both hands, which pushes the instrument too hard into the face and can injure the lips. "The rim of the mouthpiece is very sharp," he says. "It's like a cookie cutter going into dough." Mr. Burns advises keeping the inward pull of the instrument to an absolute minimum—just enough to keep the instrument in place, so that the inward pull is delicately balanced with the outward push from the air flow and the lip cushion.

Mr. Burns also advises letting the right little finger rest on top of the finger hook, instead of putting it in the hook, to minimize hand tension (see Figures 42, 43, and 44). "You only need the hook if you're holding the instrument with one hand to turn a page or to use a mute."

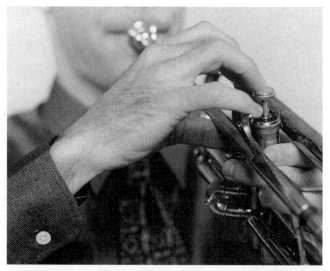

Figure 42 Letting the little finger rest on top of the hook and easing the grip on the trumpet prevents injury to the lips.

Figure 43 Keeping the little finger in the hook of the trumpet and gripping the instrument too tightly pulls the horn too hard into the face, which can injure the lips.

Figure 44 Playing with tense, flat fingers causes stiffness in the hand and arm.

Percussion

Percussionist and Alexander teacher Melanie Nevis helps players of all instruments discover the minimum amount of muscle tension they need to hold their instrument or to push down keys. Percussionists who come to her typically grip their sticks too tightly. The tension travels up into the arm and shoulder. She asks students to hold an object, such as a book, in their hand and move it through space, gradually lessening their grip. If they drop the book, they've gone too far and can then experiment with finding the minimum grip needed to hold the book without excess tension.

Retraining Your Hands

Learning to let go of tension takes mental, not physical, effort. Once a muscle is tightened, the only way to release it is to *allow* it to release. You can't make the muscle release by using additional muscular effort.

Teachers who retrain musicians ask them to limit their practice time so that they can work with great mental focus. If the student is recovering from an injury, some teachers limit practice time to as little as fifteen minutes a day. Others suggest practicing only ten minutes at a time so that the mind is fresh and alert. Whether you have had an injury or not, in order to program new movement patterns into the nervous system, each move you make must be done with as much awareness as possible. Work slowly, paying attention to one movement at a time without anticipating the next move. As you practice, the new way of moving will take less and less conscious effort to maintain. Eventually, it will become automatic—a new habit that replaces the old one.

If you are recovering from a practice-related injury, it is

most important to notice when your muscles begin to feel slightly tired and to stop at that point. If you push yourself further, you may experience pain and reinjure yourself.

Wrist Flexibility and Position

The fingers enable us to handle objects with precision and refined control. The wrist, arm, and shoulder serve to position the hand in space. Their high degree of mobility suits this purpose well.

The wrist contains eight bones that roll around against one another like marbles, providing tremendous flexibility.[3] Each instrument requires the wrist to be used in a different way. Some require much more movement than others, and some require using the wrist primarily in a neutral position—that is, a position of balance in which the wrist doesn't bend in any particular direction. Whether the wrist bones are mobile or stabilized, the wrist functions as a dynamic bridge that allows energy to flow between the fingers and the forearm.

EXTREME POSITIONS

Performing arts physicians find that musicians who repeatedly bend their wrist into extreme positions often develop carpal tunnel syndrome—an injury in which forearm muscles become so tense that they put pressure on a main nerve leading into the hand, causing numbness and incoordination.[4]

Piano

Sitting too low at the piano requires the forearm to reach upward to the keyboard. The wrist must therefore maintain a high position to place the fingers at an advantageous angle for depressing the keys. This constant flexion of the wrist causes strain and prevents energy from flowing naturally from the arm into the hand.

Some pianists drop the wrist below a neutral position at times. (Figure 30, on page 98, shows the neutral position of the wrist.) Dropping the wrist below this level requires your hand to reach upward to the keys even if you are sitting at the proper height. In addition to making the fingers overwork, this position stresses the wrist.

These problems are common with computer users as well. Many corporations have been served multimillion-dollar lawsuits because they did not provide workers with properly designed chairs, desks, and computer accessories, requiring employees to work in uncomfortable positions that resulted in hand and arm injuries.

To prevent such strain at the piano, sit at the proper height, as discussed on pages 97 and 98, and avoid dropping your wrist below keyboard level. Although the wrist may be raised momentarily at times, it must not be held statically in a raised position. Proper movement of the wrist is discussed on pages 118 through 123 and pages 125 through 129.

Trumpet

Trumpeter Stephen Burns says some players hold their elbows up too high, which requires the wrist to extend to an extreme degree. As with other instruments, this position interrupts the smooth flow of energy from the shoulders, causing strain (see Figures 43 and 44). He advises using "a simple, flat wrist, creating a gentle bridge of fingers, wrist, and arm" (see Figure 42).

Violin and Viola

Violinist Frances Magnes describes an opposite problem that some violinists have in holding the bow: They drop the elbow, which requires the wrist to flex too far. This position destroys the connection through the whole arm into the bow, making it difficult to control the sound and the direction of the bow. A properly positioned elbow and wrist allow the player to modulate the degree of pressure on the string easily as she moves back and forth from the tip of the bow, which requires more pressure, to the frog, which requires less pressure.

STIFFNESS IN A NEUTRAL POSITION
Holding the wrist stiffly in a neutral position can also cause tension or injury.

Guitar
Guitarist Patrick O'Brien advises sometimes holding the wrist in position "with gentle firmness" rather than locking it into one place. "If I ask you to lock it," he says, "you will probably hook the tips of your fingers and lock your whole arm."

Flute
Janet Weiss says many flute players overdo the basic flute technique of keeping the wrist steady and fail to move it to reach distant keys. Relying solely on stretching their fingers to the side, they injure the tendons in those fingers.

Piano
Using the hand in an extremely stretched position on the keyboard can be overly strenuous if the wrist is not slightly raised. Letting the wrist move up also allows arm muscles to work easily. The arm provides needed power that can't be produced by finger movement alone. In an old school of piano technique, teachers put a coin on the back of a student's hand and punished him if it fell off, because it meant the wrist had moved. I often see pianists who are unaccustomed to moving their wrists. Once they learn how to move them properly, their playing opens up due to the increased flow of energy into their hands. In later sections I'll describe specific ways of using the arm and letting the wrist move naturally.

String Instruments

The importance of wrist flexibility was dramatically illustrated in a violin master class given by Yehudi Menuhin in New York. Some of the students had been taught to hold the bow with their thumb flat, which causes stiffness through the wrist while bowing. He had them bend the thumb slightly, which allows the wrist to move freely. The results amazed me: This small adjustment of the thumb freed the entire playing mechanism, unleashing the musical power of each player. Every phrase expanded into a huge arc of sound that filled the hall. (Karen Ritscher demonstrates these two ways of using the thumb in Figures 45 and 46.)

Frances Magnes points out that the violinist's left wrist must also bend to different degrees. As the hand shifts position up the fingerboard, especially above fourth position, you need to "push the wrist out," she says, or flex it away from the instrument, so that the fingers can reach the strings. She calls this position "being on top of the fiddle." It allows you to maintain your hold on the instrument with your thumb while reaching far up on the strings with your other fingers.

ULNAR DEVIATION

Many instrumentalists habitually strain their hands out to the side. A professional accompanist came to his first lesson with me suffering from tendinitis (painful, inflamed tendon and muscle) at the base of his thumb due to the habit of bending his wrist sideways toward the little finger. Known as "ulnar deviation" (because the hand deviates toward the outer forearm bone, the ulna), this position puts great strain on the thumb side of the wrist. When he learned to raise his wrist slightly to accomplish wide stretches, he stopped turning his hand so far sideways and his pain subsided.

Other instrumentalists develop the same problem. According to Dr. Richard Norris:

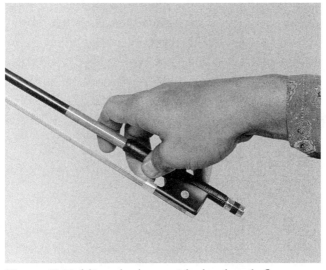

Figure 45 Holding the bow with the thumb flat causes stiffness in the wrist, limiting movement.

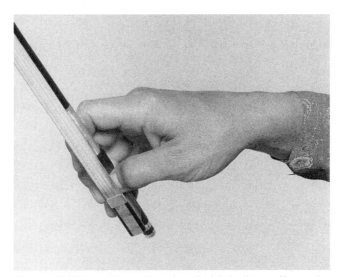

Figure 46 Using a bent thumb to hold the bow allows the wrist to move easily so that energy from the arm can transfer directly into the bow and onto the strings.

String players should be careful to avoid a position of extreme ulnar deviation in the wrist when playing up-bow at the frog. The acute flexion of the left wrist occurring during big stretches or in the highest positions on the "chin strings" [violin and viola] also causes the tendons to pull around a sharp angle, with a resulting increase in friction. Ulnar deviation is common in percussionists, . . . the right hands of electric-bass guitarists, and the right hands of harpists in the high positions unless the right elbow is held up (abducted) as in the Salzedo technique. Not all instrumentalists will develop this problem, but there are certain occupational hazards.[5]

Janet Weiss says that one of the main problems in playing a flute that does not fit your hands is that it requires too much ulnar deviation. Redesigning your instrument to make it more user-friendly (as described earlier) can eliminate this problem (see Figures 40 and 41, on page 108).

Using the Arm and Wrist to Help the Fingers

The arm is heavier and stronger than the fingers, so it provides a great deal of power. Imagine trying to lift a heavy object or make a loud sound on a piano with finger exertion alone. Such excessive strain is unnecessary. Even soft sounds on a piano are often best created by using the force or weight of the arm to help out the fingers.

To understand the difference between finger leverage and arm leverage, use a keyboard to play the same series of notes (or play on a table, imagining the keys) in three different ways:

1. Use only finger flexion (bending) to press the keys.
2. Without bending the fingers, move the arm forward and back, letting the wrist move up and down. The finger

functions as an extension of the arm, and the movement of the arm makes the key go down.

3. Use a combination of fingers and arm, bending the fingers normally and letting the arm move forward and back so that the wrist moves up and down.

Most of the time, combining finger and arm movement is easiest and most natural because all the levers of the playing mechanism share the work.

Traversing Keyboard and Fingerboard

The forward movement of the arm, and consequent raising of the wrist, is particularly useful when transferring the weight of the arm from a long finger—such as the index or middle finger—to a shorter one—such as the ring or little finger.[6]

Piano
Try balancing your arm weight on your third finger on a table, or on a white key of a keyboard instrument. Let your arm "stand" on that finger, shifting the weight of the arm from side to side to feel that the weight is balanced on the fingertip.

Then shift your arm weight to the fourth finger and notice how the arm has to move forward to balance on the shorter finger, raising the wrist (see Figure 47). The wrist doesn't need to move very much to give you the feeling of "standing" on the finger. Moving the wrist up too far weakens the connection between arm and hand. You want to feel a firmness in the fingertip that comes from the weight of the arm dropping into it, and a connection between the shoulder blade and the fingertip. Rather than statically holding the wrist up away from the pull of gravity, let the wrist respond dynamically to the movement of

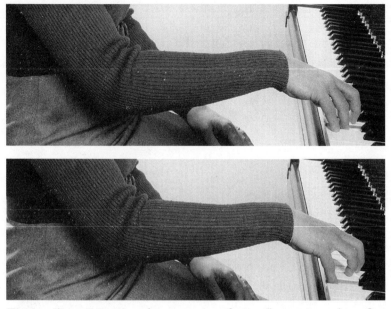

Figures 47 & 48 Letting the arm move forward to assist a short finger, such as the fourth, in pushing down a piano key may raise the wrist momentarily above the arch of the hand. In transferring arm weight from the fourth finger to the fifth, which is even shorter, the arm must move forward farther, causing the wrist to move even higher. *Keeping the wrist in a raised position, however, causes strain.*

the finger so that the impact of pushing the key travels through the wrist into the forearm and is distributed through the entire length of the arm.

Finally, transfer your arm weight to the fifth finger. Notice that the arm and wrist move still farther (see Figure 48).

By using this technique you lighten the load on your fingers and keep energy flowing through your wrist. Do not keep the wrist in a raised position, but let it move naturally in response to the movement of the fingers.

This shift of arm weight also works for moving to black keys because they are farther back on the keyboard.[7] Select a passage that uses both black and white keys on the piano and experiment with this movement of the arm. It's like navigating across the terrain of the keyboard, being aware of the ups and downs of your hand and of the topography.

Maureen tried this technique at her lesson but couldn't get the hang of it. Then she suddenly exclaimed with a big smile, "Oh, *I* see! It's like *walking* on the keys!" This is an accurate description. When you walk, you transfer the weight of your body from one foot to the other. Because the fingertips are curved and together form a curved line, if you are playing fast it feels more like *rolling* over the keys. This walking or rolling sensation in playing is comfortable and provides a feeling of intimacy with your instrument. The hand feels molded to the contours of the keyboard.

Cello

Cellist Jeffrey Solow uses the word "walking" to describe left-hand technique for his instrument:

> The left arm functions, to a large extent, by "walking" on its fingers. In actual walking, torso balance shifts forward, whereupon it is caught on top of the moving legs. Similarly, when the balance of the upper arm shifts, it must be caught by another finger or the arm will fall over. [You] can feel this by "walking" [your] arm along a tabletop or along the back of a chair. This walking image can be strengthened by imagining that the fingerboard is a staircase and the fingers stand on the horizontal surfaces of the steps. Picturing this helps [you] feel that [your] balance is aligned vertically in the earth's gravity even though [your] fingers look angled back in relation to the surface of the fingerboard.[8]

Springing, Buoyancy, and Feedback

Piano

If you are "walking" your arm *slowly* across a keyboard, try springing gently from your fingertips to propel the arm forward. This movement is similar to springing from your feet when you walk: Instead of relying exclusively on big hip and thigh muscles to lift your feet off the ground, you also engage smaller muscles, of the lower legs and the feet. Initiating a movement with a smaller body part distributes the labor, making the movement more efficient.

In the springing motion, the finger grasps the key (you can feel this on a table just as well), pushing against it and propelling the arm upward and forward while you hold the key down. This technique is easier and more natural than pushing the arm forward from the shoulder or upper arm. It is similar to what swimmers do when they reach the end of a swimming pool and turn around to swim back: They push off from the side of the pool by springing from their feet. Springing creates momentum, it feels good, and it provides a change of pace from other types of movement.

When you spring from the surface of a key, your initial contact with the instrument is soft and sensitive because you focus on the cushiony sensation in the fingerpad (the fleshy part of the fingertip) rather than on exertion of the upper arm and shoulder. Joan Campbell Whitacre describes the difference this way: "You need big, powerful arm and shoulder muscles primarily to position the arm and hand so that the fingers can make contact with the instrument. When you work harder with these muscles than this action requires, your intention is to be powerful. But when you initiate from the fingertips, your intention is to touch the instrument with the feeling of the music and to work from that sensation into a gradual recruitment of the power needed to fully express the feeling. The result is a more sensitive touch. It's mechanically efficient and can be as powerful as it needs to be, but it remains sensitive."

Because springing forward from the fingertips provides a great deal of power with minimum effort, it's an easy way to make a loud sound on the piano. It also allows you to easily play two or more keys at a time with one hand. Try playing a chord using only finger movement; you will notice it's somewhat difficult. Then play the same chord using arm movement to help the fingers; it will be easier. The slight grip of the fingertips creates a penetrating sound. The looseness of the arm makes the sound full and relaxed as well.

Because springing gives you power, it helps in shaping phrases. In a simple two-note phrase, for example, you can easily create a decrescendo by springing on the first note and simply pressing the second key with your finger. The energy of the spring will carry your hand to the end of the phrase and help to create a legato effect.

Springing frequently works well also in playing long notes because it allows you to keep moving instead of freezing in place. Occasional, well-placed springs in a slow melody help you keep a sense of continuity.

Springing makes the arm feel buoyant, and pleasant vibrations from contacting the instrument feed back into the body. Be sure to maintain a sense of connection between your fingertips and your shoulder blade so that the energy can flow freely through the arm in both directions.

Try springing your fingertips on a tabletop and notice the effect on your arm and body. It's like walking with a spring in your step—the energy from pushing against the ground with your feet feeds back into your feet and through your legs. You feel solid and supported by the ground, but also light. Springing from your fingertips gives your instrumental technique the lightness and precision of a cat springing from its feet.

Staccato on the Piano—A Variant of Springing

Staccato is often best accomplished on the piano by springing the hand and arm up off the keys, which I call "bouncing."

The fingertip initiates the bounce by grasping or "biting" the key and propelling the arm straight up, just as you would jump with your feet from a trampoline. This movement is easier than brushing the key with the fingertip (moving the finger toward the palm of the hand), as pianists sometimes do. You simply let the whole arm bounce up from the keys, and then let it drop so that the hand lands on the keys in position for the next note before playing it.

To learn this technique, think "bounce, land" with every note. Landing means letting your fingers rest on the keys after every note instead of holding tension in the hand by keeping the fingers in the air. It economizes on movement: Instead of playing a note and then searching for the next key, you aim for the next key when you bounce off the first one, and you go directly to it.

Buoyancy in Bowing and Drumming

Buoyancy also occurs in playing other instruments. Karen Ritscher describes the string player's bow arm as buoyant. She devised a technique of using giant rubber bands (purchased in athletic supply stores) to wrap around a viola student's shoulder and forearm, giving the sensation of buoyancy in the arm. It's a way of learning how gravity and uplifted energy play against each other, providing ease and pleasure in movement.

Frances Magnes teaches a balanced use of pressure and release in bowing. One technique she teaches is to begin a stroke with a "bite"—to press harder than usual at the frog and then release the pressure as soon as you start moving the bow. "That makes for a very clean, precise beginning," she says. The bite gives the sound a sharp, focused quality. The release gives it a fullness and warmth.

Drummer Richard Sylvester says proper stick technique

has a buoyant quality. Holding the stick close to the drum-head, you direct the striking action away from your body and the drumhead so that the striking point is not the end-point of the action but is just one point in an arc. With this technique, the arm feels buoyant and free. "If you just hit downward with the stick, it's dead," he says. The drumhead does not vibrate as musically. Try these two approaches using a pencil on a table to feel the difference.

Buoyancy, Support, and the Circulation of Energy

If your instrument rests on the floor while you play it, like a piano or a cello, the instrument provides a degree of physical support for the body. When springing or bowing, instead of just going through the motions with your hands and arms, tune into the energy that comes back into your body from the instrument. Laban Movement Analyst Martha Eddy describes a cello or a piano as "a very fancy cane, in some ways," that supports the body. Feel how your arms would just fall down-ward if the instrument were not there to support them. Give in to gravity and let the instrument support you. The arms will then relax, and movement will feel effortless.

The arrows marked on the photos in Figure 49 show how springing allows energy to circulate freely through the body.

1. The force of gravity on your entire body counterbalances
2. the upward force on the fingertips when the piano keys hit bottom.
3. Springing from the fingertips to propel the arm upward and forward sends an impulse from the fingertips up the arm and
4. down the spine.
5. This impulse reaches the sit bones, sending a counter

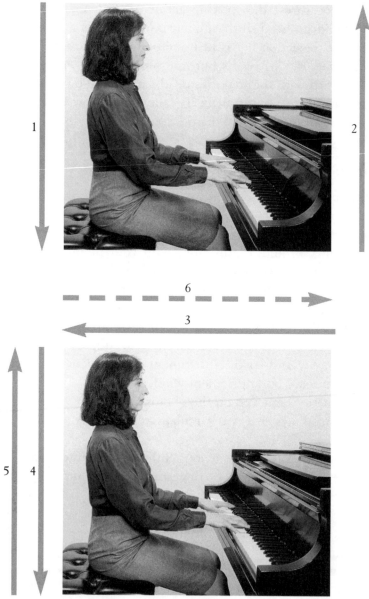

Figure 49

impulse up from the seat. The counterimpulse continues upward through the spine and

6. forward through the arm.

Energy thus circulates continuously through the body.

Joan Campbell Whitacre describes this free give and take of energy as similar to a handshake: "You can shake someone's hand as much to receive what they're giving to you as to give what you're offering to them. Then you take something into you from them, and the communication is more complete."

Rotation

Many instruments, including piano and string instruments, require a forearm movement called "rotation." This is the movement we make when turning a doorknob. To understand how rotation works, extend your forearm in front of you with the palm facing up. Then turn the arm over so that the palm faces down. Figure 50 shows that when the palm of the hand faces up, the two forearm bones— the radius and the ulna—are parallel. As the palm turns downward, the radius rotates around the ulna so that the two bones cross to form an X.

Place your left hand on your right forearm bones at the wrist to feel how this rotation happens. Notice that only the forearm seems to shift position, not

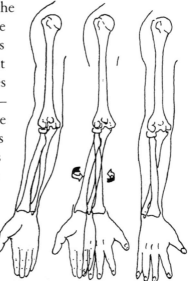

Figure 50

the upper arm. But if you press against the upper arm bone while doing the rotation, you will notice that it moves slightly also.

Notice that when the two forearm bones are parallel, there is considerable space between them. This space is occupied by various muscles, tendons, and connective tissues. Although this space changes shape when the radius rotates around the ulna to bring the two bones into an "X" relationship, it does not close up. Therefore, during rotation, focus on maintaining this space to allow the forearm muscles to remain relaxed.

Piano

The springing motion on the piano often involves some degree of forearm rotation. For example, if you transfer your arm weight from the tip of your third finger to the tip of your fourth or fifth finger, the arm has to move toward that outer corner of your hand. This diagonal movement combines the forward spring with a rotation of the forearm. The forearm rotates out to the side, changing the angle of the palm of the hand.

The example of piano music below (Example 1) is marked with arrows indicating where a springing motion is used. The third, fourth, and fifth arrows mark notes that require a diagonal springing motion, which includes rotation of the arm.

Example 1
Mozart: Piano Sonata in D Major, K. 284, 3rd mvt.

Pure rotation, uncombined with any forward movement of the arm, is also an important technique. In Example 2, subtle springing motions are used to negotiate the eighth notes (spring on the notes played by the fourth finger) while rotation accomplishes a clear melodic line in the same hand.

Example 2
Schubert: Impromptu in G Flat, Opus 90, No. 3

Rapid back-and-forth rotation of the arm accomplishes brilliant trills and tremolos. It is the only repetitive movement the body can make that is as fast as the finger trill. Getting the arm into the act gives trills much more power.

String Instruments

String players, particularly violinists and violists, have to rotate their left forearm to position the hand on the fingerboard. Violinist Frances Magnes says that when the player's forearm is not sufficiently rotated, the fingers come down on the wrong places on the strings, resulting in poor intonation. When a violinist learns to hold the instrument with a more rotated forearm, the fingers are more likely to fall where they need to for playing in tune. Ms. Magnes teaches her students that in a good position "they should be able to see just a little bit of their elbow" when they look down. "Overdone is as bad as underdone," she says. "If you rotate too far, your arm gets tight and you feel like you're tying yourself into knots."

The bow arm also needs to rotate. "Every stroke has a depth to it," says Karen Ritscher. "You go into the string, and as you lean your weight into the tip of the bow, the radius rotates around the ulna. If you just drop your weight vertically into the string, you get a squawky sound. The string can't vibrate, so you kill the sound. But if you use rotation to move the bow, the stroke has more elasticity and produces a freer sound."

"Dropping in" with the Arm

In buoyant movements like springing, we use our muscles to counteract gravity. Often we need to know how to take advantage of gravity instead. We take gravity for granted. But think how powerful and all-pervasive it is—without it we'd go floating off into space, along with pianos, cellos, cars, and everything else that's not attached to the ground.

In transferring arm weight from one finger to another (the "walking" movements described earlier for pianists and cellists), we use gravity to move efficiently over the keyboard or fingerboard. Gravity can also serve us well when we make larger arm movements.

Piano and String Instruments

Bowing a string instrument or eliciting a ringing sound from a piano often works best when, instead of working hard with the arm, you just let the weight of the arm drop into the instrument. Instead of pushing the strings or keys, you use gravity to make them play, with just enough muscular effort to hold the arm at the most effective angle and control the force of the drop.[9]

To drop freely, the arm has to be loose. Try lifting your arms up and then tightening the muscles; it becomes impossible to drop your arms. To let them drop toward your instrument, you need to release the muscles. Then the arms will fall automatically.

Frances Magnes puts her hand under a violin student's forearm and asks him to rest the weight of his arm in her hand in order to feel how the forearm can drop freely into the bow and onto the strings. "If you're not resting the arm on something," she says, "it's hard to get a sense of its weight." Releasing the forearm this way while bowing produces a round, full sound, whereas pushing hard with the arm results in a tight, brittle sound.

When a pianist has difficulty letting the arm drop freely, I suggest the following exercise. Sit upright on a firm seat and place the palm of your hand, fingers open, on your thigh. Make a few quick gripping motions with the fingers to get a sense of the spring power in your hand. Now spring your whole arm straight up into the air and let it fall back down. If your arm is very loose, your hand will spring easily above the level of your head and fall fast and hard with a smack on your leg. If it's tight, it will resist the spring and fall with less force. Repeating the exercise a few times can help loosen the arm.

Paul used this exercise to loosen his arm for playing a Chopin waltz. Before doing the exercise, his playing sounded restrained. When he played again after doing the exercise, the piano rang with such fullness that it sounded like a different instrument. He looked at his arm in awe, wondering where this powerful, new limb had come from.

Experimenting with Different Arm Techniques

You need a teacher to guide you in applying these techniques to a variety of musical passages. When working with arm movement on your own, try to feel a healthy balance between mobility and stability of the wrist. If the wrist is too loose, the line of energy from the arm into the hand is broken. If it's too tight, the flow of energy toward the fingers stops at the wrist.

Getting stuck in any one pattern of using the arm overtaxes one group of muscles, creating tension that can lead to injury. As in any other physical activity, it doesn't feel good to do the same thing over and over. Paying attention to how you feel, varying your movements, and taking frequent breaks to stretch and relax are the best insurance against unpleasant and possibly harmful practicing.

Special Issues for Voice and Wind Instruments

Minimum Tension in the Mouth, Jaw, Throat, and Tongue

Gripping, grabbing, and straining are not limited to the hands and arms. For singers and wind players, learning to use the tongue, throat, and facial muscles with ease and efficiency is a challenge. According to voice teacher Jeannette Lovetri, part of the difficulty is in changing the habits formed in daily living: "In this culture people hold tremendous tension in their necks, shoulders, jaws, and tongues," she says. Watching this habit as you go about your day can help you loosen up in these places.

Voice

Because the muscles of the throat, tongue, and jaw are all interconnected, tension in one of these parts affects the entire area. Voice teacher James Carson says that many singers are taught that they should feel nothing happening in the throat while singing, so they make a special effort not to use the muscles of the throat, which only creates tension in them. Instead, a singer needs to develop an awareness of the muscles in the throat and use them properly.

To develop such awareness, Mr. Carson teaches singers to "think the sound" they want to produce and then notice how their vocal mechanism automatically moves, in response to that thought, to make the sound. If you think the sound "guh," for example, you can feel movement in the back of your throat as the vocal cords prepare to produce the sound. "You can sense the exact spot on your vocal cords from which each pitch will generate," Mr. Carson says. This method, which allows a singer to control both pitch and timbre, comes from the Old Italian School of singing taught in the nineteenth century by such masters as Antonio Cotogni, who trained the great tenor Beniamino Gigli. The method carried over into Germany, where soprano Lilli Lehmann learned and taught it. Because this approach allows the vocal mechanism to respond naturally to a singer's intentions, it helps prevent excessive effort in producing correct pitch and a good sound.

Just as minimum left-hand tension gives string players the sensitivity to play in tune, minimum tension in the vocal mechanism allows singers to sing in tune. Voice teacher Jeannette Lovetri points out that when the muscles in the throat are stiff and inflexible, the vocal cords cannot stretch and thin out easily enough to produce higher pitches, so notes are frequently flat.

Mr. Carson explains that when the vocal mechanism is working properly, the vocal cords (or folds), which resemble a rubber band, "zip up" partially, from back to front, as the pitch is raised, so that the opening between the cords gets smaller and tighter. Tension in the vocal mechanism prevents the cords from zipping up properly, so that the pitch produced lacks overtones, making it sound out of tune. When such inefficient use occurs, singers have no choice but to compensate by pushing too hard with the breathing muscles to get a bigger and better sound. This "overblowing" works against the already misused vocal cords by overwhelming them with air; the air blows through the gap in the portion of the cords that should be zipped up, resulting in irritation and possible swelling. This swelling allows the cords to rub against each other, which irritates the cords even more and can create a blister (or nodule) and eventually a callus (or node). A node makes singing difficult and makes it impossible to produce a clear sound. Overblowing also causes the vocal cords to bow out and get too long, making the pitch sharp.

Mr. Carson finds that when the mechanism in the throat functions properly, it has a beneficial effect on the entire body. Not only is the singer less inclined to push too hard with the breathing muscles, but because tension in the neck is released, posture improves, automatically making breathing easier. Released muscles also create greater resonance because (1) they allow musical vibrations to travel through the bones more freely, and (2) they allow the body cavities to expand. The sound resonates not just from the throat but from the whole body.

Woodwinds and Brass Instruments

Flutist Janet Weiss shares this understanding of how resonance is created. "You can't be tight and have range of color," she says. She describes a chain reaction of tension starting in the neck and jaw, leading to tonguing problems, which cause embouchure problems, which in turn cause difficulties with breathing and with sound.

Ms. Weiss explains that the inside of the mouth should be very open because it's the resonating chamber, or "sound board." A stiff tongue binds up the sound board and the playing mechanism. Tonguing with too much force or tension creates an unpleasant sound. Trumpeter Stephen Burns says many trumpet players use what he calls a "zucchini tongue"—a tensed, cylindrical tongue position that is not fluid and flexible. As in flute playing, this tension makes articulation difficult.

According to Janet Weiss, flutists who pull their embouchure muscles too tightly can get TMJ (temporomandibular joint) syndrome—a debilitating tension in the jaw. TMJ syndrome also afflicts saxophone players who grip their instrument too hard with their teeth. Ms. Weiss says that a less-than-ideal instrument can easily contribute to such tension. A flute may have a head joint that is too hard to blow. An oboe or bassoon may have a reed "like a Popsicle stick"—incapable of producing much sound. She recommends using a high-quality instrument to avoid such problems.

Breathing

Overtightening the abdominal muscles is a frequent breathing problem among singers and wind players. James Carson explains that in singing, each change of pitch requires a change in air pressure, which is created by movement in the chest and abdomen. If the abdominal or chest muscles are rigid, they cannot move easily or quickly enough to produce these changes.

Flutists need to take in a great deal of air to play their instrument because they blow air across the mouthpiece instead of directly into it. If the abdominals are too tight, the player cannot take in enough air.

According to Stephen Burns, power in trumpet playing comes not from forcing the breath through tight lips but from allowing the muscles in the torso to move freely and from releasing the throat and facial muscles so that they will naturally align and create a free vibration. It's a question of "coordination and relaxation," he says—"identifying more with the flow rather than the force generating it."

Mr. Burns also says that many players "clutch the breath": They take a breath and hold it before blowing out. Often, "it's out of fear of what's going to come out—wanting it to be perfect." But some players hold the breath to create a certain amount of compression when they blow. Mr. Burns feels that this practice goes against the natural rhythm of the breath and creates unnecessary tension. He recommends working consciously with the in-and-out rhythm of the breath to develop ease, coordination, and confidence in releasing the sound.

CONCLUSION

Musicians often confuse being emotionally intense with being physically tense. Intense expressiveness and power come not from overtightening the physiological mechanism that produces the sound but from freeing that mechanism to work smoothly and efficiently.

If you begin with a posture that organizes the body to function at maximum efficiency and strength, and use your playing or singing mechanism to best mechanical advantage, your vital energies can flow directly into your instrument and create a rich, vibrant sound. In this state of minimum tension, repeating a passage doesn't feel purely repetitive; you begin to notice slight variations each time because your body is free to express itself spontaneously.

See what happens if you allow your body to relax and open up. Get acquainted with its subtle rhythms and energies. Let yourself discover the ease and joy of natural movement.

CHAPTER 7

The Spark of Inquisitiveness

Step Five: Follow your curiosity as you practice.

Jessica was one of several students who gathered at my studio one evening for their first experience of performing for a group. She had carefully practiced the difficult sections of her Bartók piece and had planned to focus on them during her performance. But as she sat nervously on the bench facing the gleaming row of black and white keys, it all escaped her. She couldn't remember anything about the piece except which keys to touch first. Suddenly, she buried her face in her hands and exclaimed, half-laughing and half-crying, "It's amazing. Everything just goes out the window."

After a few moments, she regained her composure and began to play. Although her performance contained a few more mistakes than usual, it was more vibrant than anything I had heard from her at her lessons. She didn't know quite what had happened, but her face radiated victory.

Something takes over in performance. Whatever we have thought about in preparing the piece is flooded out of our mind by a great stream of energy. We give this energy many names—"flow," "spontaneity," "right-brain activity," "alpha waves." By whatever name, it is the energy of our wild, free self let loose. We feel its power regardless of our ability to handle it or of the quality of our performance.

This freedom can also reign during practice. You can cultivate spontaneity by paying attention to what you want to practice and by working in a way that interests you. This is *Step Five: Follow your curiosity as you practice.*

Practicing can proceed without a rigid plan. You don't have to do things in the same order as yesterday or pick up where you left off in your last session. You don't always have to start with the most difficult section or practice every tricky passage three or ten or fifty times in a row. Hidden under such rigid programming is the voice of creative intelligence. You can listen to that voice; you can follow it and see where it leads you.

To do this, simply ask yourself, "What do I want to do now?" Then do it. Ask it frequently. If you're not accustomed to listening to your inner voice, it might take a while to hear what it's saying. But if you keep listening, your intuition will begin to develop and take you on a creative journey. One of my students remarked that by working in this way he stumbled across many more exciting details in music than he ever discovered by sticking to a plan.

It isn't capricious to say, "I feel like practicing *this* piece now," or "I'm tired of working on this. I want to practice a different piece." On the contrary, in following your interest, you honor your intelligence. Do you always take the same route to the grocery store, or do you sometimes feel like going a different way? It might perk you up to see a different series of buildings for a change. Or you might spot a tree newly in flower.

Do you want to look at the fingering in bar three? The phrasing on page six? Go ahead. Do you feel like stopping and taking a rest for a minute? Fine. Then ask yourself again, "What interests me now?" Take as much time as you need to listen for the answer within you. Maybe you feel like getting your fingers into a big chordal section. Or maybe you'd rather handle a more delicate passage. As long as it holds your interest, your work will be fresh and creative.

We can't develop spontaneity for performing if we spend hours every day controlling ourselves. Even with all the stops and starts inherent in practicing, we need a feeling of continuity and flow. The continuity of practicing lies not in playing a piece through from beginning to end but in staying with our mind, being true to our own intelligence, from the beginning to the end of a practice session.

If you want to play a piece through in its entirety, go ahead. But don't let that prevent you from stopping in the middle if you suddenly feel attracted to a particular phrase. It might be a little scary to let go of plans, but you can trust your own mind.

Resistance

Everyone has moments, or days, when they don't feel like practicing but know they must. When resistance comes up, be gentle with yourself. Like many musicians, you may notice that most of your resistance is simply against making the trip over to the instrument and facing the work that awaits. Once you put yourself in position to practice, resistance usually begins to dissolve.

Proceed slowly and gently from whatever state of mind you're in. If you fight the resistance by dragging yourself over to the instrument and forcing yourself to practice, you create tension and are likely to feel even more resistant than before. Instead, let yourself feel the resistance, and then slowly take one step at a time toward the instrument and take your time getting started. See if anything arouses your curiosity. It can be something as simple as how your hands feel that day. Try placing them on the instrument. Notice how they feel. Play one note or a few notes. See what each movement feels like. By relaxing with your resistance, you can gently break it down.

Balance

Sometimes we're afraid that if we just do what we want, we'll practice only the music we can play well and we'll never get around to tackling passages that really need work. It's a question of balance. Intuitively, you know what you need to do. You may wish you could spend all your time on a particular piece, but you know you can't. Avoiding responsibility doesn't feel good. It's like eating an unbalanced diet. If you overindulge in eating chocolate, sooner or later you get sick from loading up on sugar and cocoa and you long to feel healthier.

Look for a balance between avoiding your work and compulsively trying to perfect a difficult passage. If you force yourself to go over something a hundred times in a row, gritting your teeth and saying, "I'm going to get it no matter what," you will wear yourself out. Instead, try practicing the passage three or four times, then take a break and work on something easier for a while.

If you respect your teacher and he has set guidelines for structuring your practice time, follow those guidelines as closely as you can. But by occasionally experimenting with a slightly different approach, you can understand the value of your teacher's approach better, and your work will become more intelligent. As a student, you needn't try to be a carbon copy of your teacher; you need to cultivate your own intelligence, both for your own practice and so that you will have enough understanding to perhaps teach others someday. Intelligent teachers don't do everything that *their* teachers told them to do. They have found out from their own experience what works best for them, and they know you must do the same. Furthermore, a good teacher continues to learn as he teaches and is open to students' ideas.

Deadlines

If you have a deadline, such as an upcoming concert or a lesson the next day, you will naturally want to focus on whatever you have to present at that time. But be careful to notice when you start to lose interest, and don't continue unless you think you can regain your interest and do productive work. The only time I ever followed a strict plan was the day or two before a concert. I tape recorded my playing, listened to the tape, and made a note of missing elements: "Bar 17: remember crescendo. Bar 19: left hand unclear." Then I would systematically practice each of those places, knowing I had only a limited amount of time. In a situation like that, your intuitive intelligence is still in charge: It's telling you that if you don't take care of these details, the performance won't be your best.

If you practiced that way from day one of studying a piece, you would have no joy. Someone once suggested that to learn the required piece for a certain piano competition, I should photocopy my score, cut out two lines from this copy each day, and focus only on those two lines. It sounded like a logical approach, but I couldn't do it. I kept getting curious about the rest of the piece, and I was able to learn it in time by working on whatever section interested me at a particular moment.

Some deadlines are impossible to meet if you try to learn the music thoroughly. Accompanists, for instance, are sometimes hired just a few days before a concert; they don't have time to learn the program as well as they would like. Preparing music under such circumstances is an art in itself and requires that you recognize the most important aspects of a piece and bring out as much detail as you can in the time available. Appreciate your skill and your generosity in rising to the occasion for such a performance; it will help you relax and enjoy your work.

Scales

Following general guidelines for dividing your time will help you learn a variety of music. If you are studying three pieces at a time, for instance, you may want to work on each of them almost every day. But many musicians go to extremes with practice regimens. One violinist I heard about spends two hours a day on scales because she feels that in dealing with the technical issues involved, everything she needs to know becomes instinctive, which makes her feel less anxious about performing. This is an extremely time-consuming method for reducing anxiety. If you spend two hours a day on scales, you're taking too much time away from the music you need to learn.

Scales can be fun. They have an energizing, calisthenic quality, and playing them in octaves, thirds, and sixths can be an enjoyable exercise. When a child sees her piano teacher play a scale, she usually gets excited about trying it herself. Children like the idea that by moving their thumb under their other fingers they can play scales all the way up to the top of the keyboard and all the way back down. It gives them a feeling of power.

If you know the fingering for every scale, you can play it whenever you see it in a new piece without having to think. If you have time to practice scales in all twenty-four keys and you enjoy it, that's fine. Otherwise, you could perhaps work on C major one week and A minor the next.

Practicing scales can help you ease into your work gently.

Instead of charging into a practice session without warming up, which strains the body, you can amble through a few scales to loosen up. Unfortunately, many people view scales as a form of torture, and instead of loosening up, they tighten up in resistance to them.

The importance of scale practice varies according to the level of the student. If a student doesn't know how to execute a scale, she should learn at some point. But many professional musicians practice scales only occasionally. Some of my students like to work on scale technique at the end of their lessons, after they have satisfied their appetite for the repertoire they are studying. It's like eating salad: Some people prefer it before the main course; others find it refreshing after the main course. You can structure your practice time that way, too, and perhaps follow your salad of scales with a main course of Schubert and a dessert of Ravel.

In a piece of music, every scale passage has a unique meaning and context and requires a unique practice approach. It might crescendo or decrescendo or both; part of it might be legato and part staccato; and it may have changing rhythms and harmonies. You need to deal with the dynamics, the fingering, the exact length of the scale, and its place in the whole composition. Then it will be not only interesting but challenging to execute that particular scale, much more so than just playing a straight scale four octaves up and down.

If you do practice straight scales, practice them in a musical way. Change the dynamics, or even vary the phrasing or the timing. Most important, listen to each note. A scale is a fantastic thing. It's the basis of our musical language. Each note has a different psychological value, a tendency to settle or to lead to another note. Take the time to appreciate the effect of each sound. Notice how it feels in the context of the entire scale. You can discover endless possibilities by enjoying scales this way.

Regular Practice and Length of Practice Time

If you make a habit of practicing a reasonable length of time each day, you can progress steadily. But you also need to be flexible. For five years after I finished music school, I practiced five hours a day without fail, except for summer vacations. Then, one day, a friend called and asked if I would help her and a few other people put down the tile floor in her new store. This would mean a whole day out of my practicing, but I really wanted to help and it sounded like fun. So I said yes happily. Strangely enough, I got into a conversation about my work with a friend of hers who was also working on the floor, and he decided to give me money to buy a new piano. Several years later, I chose not to practice one weekend so that I could attend a meditation program. At the program I met a film-maker who decided to make a video about my work.

I'm not suggesting that every time you leave your instrument and go out to enjoy yourself, good fortune will befall you. But you can afford to be kind to others and to yourself, to be a human being. Occasionally, you might just need a rest—a "personal day," as corporations call it—a day to catch up with your personal life. And sometimes you might be exhausted or have a bad case of the flu and need to stay in bed.

Obviously, if you're giving a concert the next day, you need to be careful. But let yourself learn from experience. You might sometimes make the painful mistake of walking into a performance insufficiently prepared. Hopefully, the further you advance in your career, the more you will have learned from your mistakes and the better prepared you will be. But you can't learn how to practice without sometimes taking chances and seeing what happens. Only you can find your own way.

The amount of time you practice each day depends on your needs. If you're an amateur who works all day in an office, your practice time is limited. You may even have days when you can't find five minutes to practice. But even if you're a serious music student or a professional with ample practice time, the quality of your practicing is more important than the quantity. Practice at a time of day when you feel relatively fresh and can focus easily.

However long you choose to practice, feel free to take frequent breaks. Within a session, you can stop for a minute now and then and do nothing. It will clear your mind and relax your body. If you get stiff, you can get up and stretch for a few minutes.

Many musicians find that after forty-five minutes their brain needs a ten- or fifteen-minute rest. The body needs a rest, too, a change of position and a break from activity. Don't try to practice for too long without such a break. During your break it's usually best not to do anything that requires much effort. You can walk around, lounge on a comfortable couch, drink some tea, or pet your dog or cat. The body and mind require regular refreshment.

QUESTIONS AND ANSWERS

Question: *Is this intuitive approach more appropriate after you've done some preliminary work on a piece, like just learning the notes?*

Answer: This approach applies from the very beginning. When a piece is brand new, practicing might progress note by note, but you can still follow your interest. That may mean experimenting with different fingerings, seeing how they feel in your hand. Or perhaps taking a break from the new piece and working on something you know better—in which you have more of an opportunity to make music. Later on in your study, you may find that the piece that was once new has become so familiar that it sounds automatic and glib; your heart's not in it anymore. Then you may want to take the music apart note by note to hear it afresh.

When you are first learning a piece, you may feel very free to go from one section to another and to try all kinds of technical and musical approaches. In later stages of study, you have fewer choices because the more complete your performance becomes, the more likely you are to notice imperfections. If your phrasing isn't working, you really feel it in the later stages because by that time the piece flows fairly well, and any obstructions of that flow create frustration and demand your attention. The practice atmosphere becomes intense as the piece begins to take on a life of its own.

Question: *Do you recommend practicing scales and passages in different rhythms? I've noticed it makes my technique feel more solid and secure.*

Answer: I learned that type of practicing in music school, and it can be helpful, but it's often overused, to the neglect of more subtle and interesting types of practice. Playing a passage in rhythmic groups can jolt your mind into a new perception of the notes, because you are setting off each group with pauses before and after it. It's like putting a picture frame around one part of your environment and noticing how everything is arranged inside of it. That kind of practicing also gives your hands the experience of dealing with a small group of notes at a time, enabling you to become technically familiar with each small group and to develop efficiency in your movements.

But you have to draw the line at the point where you become desperate or driven about working that way. As long as it piques your curiosity and aids your understanding of how something is put together, it's fine. You're cultivating your connection to the music. But when you lose touch with the delight of it and get caught up in trying to imitate a machine, then you're working against yourself. Desperation feeds on itself, and joy slips away before you know it. So look for that distinction. Experiment and find out for yourself where the boundary is.

Question: *What do you think about practicing with a metronome? Sometimes I feel it helps me keep steady, to not get out of control.*

Answer: Metronomes have a place in practicing, but not a big one. They can tell you when you're veering off tempo, but that doesn't always mean you shouldn't veer off. We're human beings, not machines. Human rhythm is flexible, not mechanical. It breathes. Human pulse isn't rigid. It fluctuates. If you practice a lot with a metronome you suppress your natural rhythm. You put your human wildness in a box and rob yourself of your freedom. It's possible to rely more on your inner sense of rhythm.

Great artists feel the pulse of music unerringly, but the rhythm has vitality, the living elasticity of breath and movement. The mechanical beat of an electronic synthesizer, which is used in many recordings of rock music, is abysmally lacking in joy and vitality. The pulse is relentlessly rigid and attacks you like the sound of any other machine you may hear—in a factory or on a city street. Even fierce music needs to be fierce in a human way, not like a mechanical monster.

Occasionally it may be helpful to use the metronome to break the habit of being rhythmically unsteady, to relax a tightness that has crept into your execution of a passage and is throwing off your natural sense of rhythm. But to use a metronome this way you have to work slowly so that you can relax and let the old way of playing or singing the music gently fall apart.

Musicians often use metronomes to whip themselves into shape. They chug away, speeding up the metronome one

147

notch at a time, pushing themselves to play faster and faster. It becomes a race. If you want to use a metronome to increase speed, do it with awareness. Ask yourself, "Is this enjoyable? Am I tight or relaxed? Is this helping me go more deeply into the music or not?"

Natural rhythm comes from being physically settled, mentally relaxed, and emotionally unrepressed. The first thing you can do for your sense of rhythm is to let yourself be, to let your breathing and your body settle down before you practice. Let your natural energies follow their natural course. Later on we'll discuss specific methods for clearly feeling rhythmic patterns in the body and creating a sense of pulse.

Question: *Adults are self-conscious, but how do you teach a child to be conscious of what she's doing and to be natural? At a certain stage children become self-conscious and lose their naturalness. They start trying very hard.*

Answer: First, you can teach spontaneity by example. Whether you're teaching a child or an adult, it's similar to practicing: Relax before you teach, take time to think while you're with a student, and don't try too hard. If you're relaxed it's easier to perceive what the student needs. But if you're preoccupied with your own problems when the student comes in, you're less receptive to him. By taking care of yourself and not forcing yourself to teach in a particular way, you create an open atmosphere in which he can relax, too.

Like many teachers, I used to think that I had to provide immediate feedback and suggestions whenever a student finished playing a piece for me, or even as soon as he made a mistake in the middle. Then, at some point, I stopped forcing myself to do that. I thought, "I'm just going to sit here and wait until I really feel like saying something." Once I released myself from the whole program I had tried to follow, I found myself coming up with surprisingly insightful comments.

Usually we think, "I'm a teacher now. I must teach him the scale, then teach him such and such, watch to be sure his fingers are curved . . ." These may be good ideas, but if we program ourselves too much, we don't make full use of either our intelligence or the student's intelligence, and we drain the joy out of learning.

When I was in my twenties, I started to dislike teaching after several years, and it occurred to me that I'd better find a way to enjoy it, since it was my main source of income. I asked one of my students, who taught respiratory therapy at a hospital, if she knew of any good books about teaching. She recommended *Freedom to Learn* by Carl Rogers.

The book was a revelation. It described the teacher as a "facilitator of learning," and it stressed the importance of encouraging students to think for themselves rather than repeatedly telling them what to do. I underlined entire paragraphs and marked many passages with huge asterisks. But three weeks after reading it I realized, in the middle of a frustrating lesson with a seventeen-year-old, that I had not yet used any of the book's exciting ideas in my teaching. Following the book's approach, I suddenly asked my student, "What do you think of how you just played?" And out of her mouth came every comment that I had planned to make myself.

My teaching took a dramatic turn at that point. I realized I had been wasting a great deal of effort and underestimating the intelligence of my students. I began using this approach even with children. An eight-year-old would come out with a response like, "Well, I should have held my wrist higher, but I thought *that* part was pretty good. But then here I made this mistake . . ." Then I would say, "How could you make it better?" And she would reply, "Well, I *hate* to sit up straight, but . . ." Once I established two-way communication with my students, I began to discover who they really were, and teaching became a pleasure.

The word "education" comes from the Latin word *educere,* meaning "to draw out." We are not here just to feed information into our students but to bring out the abilities within them. When a student feels respected for her opinions and is encouraged to express herself, she opens up and makes music more easily. As she uses her own mind more and more, she learns to practice on her own with more intelligence.

Teaching this way also gives you room to make mistakes. Many teachers use prescribed methods because they're afraid they'll make mistakes if they don't. In any creative endeavor you must have room to make mistakes, to say the wrong thing sometimes. Mistakes are educational. Just as in playing music, if you make mistakes you discover your weaknesses and you have a chance to improve. You don't have to be a perfect teacher. You can say to the student, "I'm sorry. I was wrong. I was not the best teacher today." It takes guts, but it makes you more human in the student's eyes and it encourages him to be equally genuine with you.

Teaching with this kind of freedom requires tremendous discipline. I still sometimes find myself all set to point out the flaws in a student's performance and then suddenly realizing he needs to think for himself. Or I'm about to ask him what he thinks of how he played when I realize I'm ignoring my strong desire to compliment him. You need to look for what the situation requires from moment to moment, and you don't have to have answers all the time. Let answers and questions come to you, and let yourself play with the situation. It's an integration of work and play.

CHAPTER 8

Three Styles of Struggle

Step Six: Recognize three styles of struggle.

After we've stretched, settled down, opened up, and begun to practice with ease and curiosity, practicing can be quite a pleasure. But eventually we find ourselves struggling again. Our familiar habits of rushing, pushing ourselves, overemoting, and joylessly dragging through the music return.

Chapter 2, "Struggle and Freedom," described how physical tension can stem from habitual psychological tension. Sometimes, instead of being tense, we are lazy. We try to avoid the demands of the music by glossing over notes and treating the music casually. The first step in releasing ourselves from the hold of these psychological habits is to recognize them when they occur. This is *Step Six: Recognize three styles of struggle.*

The three psychological styles are (1) overstated passion, in which we cling to the music; (2) avoidance, in which we resist dealing with the music; and (3) aggression, in which we attack the music. These styles occur in practicing because they are part of our everyday behavior. They are ways in which we miss the mark with our actions, words, and thoughts: we get so carried away over a piece of good news that we walk down the street without watching where we're going and bump into a pole; we forget to take our food out of the oven and end up burning it; we speak harshly and hurt someone's feelings.

When we're in the grip of psychological habits during practicing, the feedback we get from our body, the instrument, and the music may not be so obvious as bumping into a pole or hurting someone's feelings. But the feelings of consternation and disappointment in ourselves can be just as painful. We repeat the same phrase over and over, pushing it into this shape and that, and it never feels right. Our habits are like layers of ice that numb and bury our natural musical feeling and intelligence.

1. Overstated Passion

Passion makes the world go round, and it makes us make music. But we often go overboard in expressing passion. We exaggerate the music's delicate shapes and colors so that less genuine feeling comes through. Unable to leave a simple, lyrical melody alone, we soup it up, make a big deal out of every little up and down of it, and squeeze every expressive detail for all it's worth, until the music can hardly breathe. We are making a show of our emotionalism, and we are trying to possess the piece, instead of genuinely opening up to the music and letting it pour through us and transform us.

It is like meeting someone for the first time at a cocktail party and gushing all over the place about how great it is to meet her. *"Oh,* it's so great to *meet* you!" you screech. "I've heard *so* much *about* you, and I'm just positively *thrilled* to actually be *shaking your hand!!"* Whereupon you suddenly lose your balance and spill your drink on her jacket.

In musical performance, this style is exemplified by the pianist who is so intent on getting close to her beloved instrument that her nose is an inch above the keyboard—until suddenly, she is so enraptured with the music that she begins to lean backward, her head raised toward heaven, her face utterly ecstatic, and her shoulders raised and curled inward as if she can hardly bear the exquisite sounds. This style is what prompted Arthur Rubinstein to answer the question "Where is a person's soul located?" by saying, "Judging from many pianists, it's in the right shoulder." Alexander Libermann, my piano teacher in my early teens, referred to this kind of playing as full of a lot of "feeling, with p.h." ("pheeling").

You don't have to have your nostrils poised over your instrument to be playing with overstated passion. Moving your torso even slightly forward or gripping your instrument even a little too hard with your hands can be an indication that you are indulging in a subtler form of swooning (unless the movement is in accordance with the physiological principles discussed in Chapter 6). Voice teacher James Carson says even singers "are always gripping everything." They might learn to release the "grip" in their jaw, but then they transfer the gripping effort to their feet, knees, or back. This habitual holding of tension in the body is a way of resisting the emotional deluge of the music. If we really let go and let it penetrate us to the core, we believe that we would feel overwhelmed.

Being aware of the exaggerated form of this style can help alert you to when you are only slightly overdoing it. Try acting out the style in an extreme way. Get the "pheeling" of it. Fall all over yourself and the instrument. Pause dramatically before particularly expressive notes. Overemphasize the contrast between the happy and sad words in a song. Sway. Swoon. Almost faint, it's so phabulous.

To complete the routine, you could pretend you're in the audience, and stand up and yell "Bravo! Bravo!" and rave to the person next to you, "Isn't it just *marvelous*?! It's one of the most fantastic performances I've ever *seen!*" (You might say it's one of the most fantastic performances you've ever *heard,* but

153

that would subtract importance from the magnificent visual histrionics.)

Once you've indulged to your overly passionate heart's content, try acting out a more subtle form of the style. Just squeeze the keys (or the bow or the mouthpiece) a little bit. Just swoon a little bit. See how it feels and sounds compared to the more dramatic version. Train yourself to become aware of the range of tricks we all play on ourselves when we get overheated in the flames of passion.

2. Avoidance

Constantly overdramatizing the music takes a lot of effort, so sometimes we try an opposite tack: playing it cool. We say to ourselves, "Hey, it's no big deal. Just lie back and play the notes." And that's about all that comes out. Notes.

This style is called "avoidance," because we are steering clear of all the details the passionate musician indulges in. We're trying to convince ourselves that they don't really matter. Instead of italicizing every note and peppering the score with exclamation marks galore, we leave out all punctuation from beginning to end so that any troublesome emotionalism is eradicated. Unfortunately, so is any emotion. It's like playing the piano with your legs crossed while you look out the window and think about what you're going to have for dinner.

If we go back to our example of meeting someone for the first time, in this style we look away with no expression on our face and offer a limp hand to shake, aiming it a foot away from the other person's hand because we're not looking and because we don't care anyway. Then we mumble, "Hi nicetomeetyou. Have you seen my drink? I know I left it around here somewhere..."

The pianist indulging in this style shuffles his feet and

slouches, with his head drooping, his wrists drooping, and his ears and mind definitely drooping. Notes tumble out in relentlessly boring fashion, and he couldn't care less. Yes, he's avoided exaggerating the contours. He's eliminated them. The page is covered with a vast array of different pitches, yet somehow the whole thing sounds monotone. Members of the audience glance at their watches and mull over the business of the day.

We avoid dealing with music not only when we deliberately "play it cool" but also when we simply fail to notice the richness and detail in a composition. We may think we hear it all, but we are missing something; we fail to fully appreciate every sound, shape, and texture indicated on the page. This lack of appreciation often occurs because we try, consciously or unconsciously, to avoid the responsibility of learning a piece in depth.

Such avoidance is frequently subtle: In the middle of an otherwise fine performance, we gloss over a few notes or fail to bring out a lovely change of harmony sufficiently. By adding a slight change of inflection on one note, we might brighten up the whole phrase. But if we overdo it, we're back in the heat of passionland again.

3. Aggression

Unable to take either the red heat of passion or the gray cool of avoidance, we sometimes choose a macho approach: "I know how to do this. I'm going to just *do* it. I'm going to *really* do it." We become driven and aggressive with the music, pounding it out, declaring our unassailable convictions full force. "This is the great *me* playing! And let me tell you, I know what I'm doing!" Bang! Crash! Ah, it feels so good to express ourselves at last!

Except that it starts to feel unpleasant after a while, and, ooh, my arms feel awfully tight. And it does sound rather harsh . . .

Back to our new friend, the one we are meeting for the first time: We grab her hand with both of ours, stiffen our arms till they're straight, shake her hand so hard that her whole body shakes, look her in the eye with our brow full of wrinkled sincerity and say, *"Great ta meetcha, pal!"* as we chomp our gum loudly. Then we let go of her hand and give her a good slap on the back, just to let her know how strongly we feel. Or is it how *strong* we feel? We're so busy being strong that our sensitivity seems to have escaped us. *"Great party, isn't it?! How 'bout another drink?! Oh, sorry I made ya spill it. That'll come out at the cleaners. Know any good jokes? Have ya heard the one about the guy who fell off a ladder?"*

The body language of the pianist in this style is similar: tall and tough in the saddle, with stiff arms, ironclad grip, and all the sensitivity of a grizzly bear. But boy, is he in control.

Sometimes our aggression comes out in passages in which we feel technically insecure. Consciously or unconsciously we think, "Oh, no! Here comes the big loud part! I don't know if I can do it! Help!" And in our panic, we clench our jaw and go into a general physiological gridlock from which no real music can flow. What comes out instead is the message "I feel uncomfortable here." On a less obvious level, we may panic only slightly, so that we make music, but not as freely and fluidly as we could.

Origin and Combinations of the Three Styles

Some degree of panic underlies all three styles. We are afraid not only of technically difficult passages but of musical demands and musical power. It is sometimes easier to gush out our excitement than to contain it. And it is sometimes easier to bury the music in a gray fog or a black rage than to absorb the flood of its infinitely varied, heart-melting colors.

Some musicians can be easily identified as having one main style. But most of us are a complicated blend of all three. We alternate among them, frequently resorting to one as a counterstrategy to another. For instance, when we notice that we're avoiding the expressive nuances, and the music sounds dry and dull, we sometimes pour on the sticky goo of overstated passion as an alternative. Discovering that that doesn't satisfy us either, we might cover our growing frustration and bewilderment with a false confidence and charge into the music with the heavy hand of aggression.

Sometimes we engage in more than one style simultaneously. We may hug our instrument in passionate embrace and aggressively try to force sound out of it at the same time. And in truth, whenever we stiffen up and bang out the music, we are also avoiding the contrasts in it.

Appreciating the Raw Material in Each Style

The next two chapters will provide techniques for overcoming the three styles of struggle. Meanwhile, when you catch yourself engaging in one of these modes of behavior, see it as a sign of being human and imperfect. Our habits are deeply ingrained, and we cannot get rid of them overnight. If we criticize ourselves every time we notice that we're overstating, spacing out, or pounding out a passage, we only create more frustration.

No matter how exaggerated your style may be, it is just raw material that can be refined. You may overstate your passion, but how wonderful it is that you have passion—can you imagine living without it? Working with music is an opportunity to refine your passion, to uplift it from crude grabbiness and clinging into passionate warmth and tenderness. Or you may be lazy and ignore one string of notes after another, but at least you have the ability to relax. As you practice you can wake up to the beauties of the music and mix your relaxation with alertness. Or perhaps you stab your instrument rudely, assaulting your own ears, but at least you have the capacity to be sharp and penetrating and not altogether mushy. Music can teach you to refine this sharpness so that when a brilliant, piercing sound is called for, you accomplish it with the precision of a razor knife instead of the brutality of an ax.

An appreciative attitude toward our precious raw material must include a sense of humor. Whenever we can smile about our crazy ways and realize that they're just part of being human, the heart opens, and we momentarily free ourselves from our habits. These habits will keep coming back; they are deeply ingrained, and we will be working with the same raw material for the rest of our lives. But by recognizing our habits and viewing them with humor, we gently loosen their grip on us and cultivate the intelligence and joy we need for authentic music-making.

QUESTIONS AND ANSWERS

Question: *Sometimes I get so frustrated with practicing that I feel angry. What should I do then?*
Answer: Let the anger subside before you continue. If you play in a state of anger, you'll be tense and the music will sound tense. Just let yourself feel the anger without either squelching it or expressing it—without either pretending it isn't happening or yelling at your instrument. This might be easier said than done, but the sooner you notice your anger, the easier it will be to let it dissolve.

Music is made out of big emotional energies; volcanoes

erupt in Beethoven, and storms rage in Chopin. If you practice being quiet and letting angry energy flow through you no matter how uncomfortable it is, you increase your feeling capacity, which makes you a better musician.

Question: *How can you be spontaneous when you're so busy analyzing your emotions?*

Answer: You don't have to analyze them. You can look into them if you like, but you can also just notice them. The next two steps [described in the next two chapters] are designed to help you get beyond the three styles and to make music more genuinely.

Spontaneity is a tricky concept. It's different from impulsiveness. Impulsiveness comes from habit: "I'm mad at him, so I'm going to yell." Or, "This music is problematic, so I'm going to push myself harder." That's impulsive. Spontaneity is the freedom not to follow every single impulse. We have so many impulses that if we followed all of them, we'd be making trouble everywhere we go. By noticing destructive impulses and not giving in to them, we open a space for a fresh, creative impulse to arise instead of a habitual one.

CHAPTER 9

Simplicity

Step Seven: Drop your attitudes and be simple.

When the struggle to be passionately expressive, coolly laid-back, or fiercely authoritative leaves us unsatisfied, a feeling of futility sets in. We wish we could get to the heart of the music, and we feel at a loss as to what to do next.

Usually, we view this moment of uncertainty as a moment of defeat. We feel inadequate because we can't simply make music. This self-doubt drains us of music-making energy. Instead, we could see our uncertainty as a victory. We have shed our armor of false confidence and are being our real selves.

When we see a great performer, we may assume that since she appears to be completely sure of herself, she doesn't experience such uncertainty. We don't think about the long, difficult process she went through to master the piece she is performing. And we forget that her communicative warmth and brilliance come from being vulnerable and spontaneous—that at the moment of performance she doesn't know exactly what will come out of the instrument or how the audience will react.

Wanting a smooth, finished performance, we try to avoid

the discomfort of being bewildered and out of control when we practice. We want to feel on top of the piece. But the uncomfortable moment of uncertainty is charged with vital energy that can transform us and the music we make. If we reverse our usual logic and let ourselves feel this uncertainty instead of shrinking from it, we release this vital energy. This is *Step Seven: Drop your attitudes and be simple.*

When you sense the futility of your struggle, stop and feel that moment, in between one form of struggle and the next, when you're unsure of what to do next. Let yourself feel it exactly as it is. You may notice that you feel a little disappointed in yourself; you long to feel more connected to the music. Let yourself feel that disappointment and longing. You may notice that you feel anxious not knowing how to reach your goal, not having an answer. Feel that anxiety without rushing to try another strategy. Don't fight what is happening. Be as you are.

After a few moments, approach the music again without trying to do anything special. Play or sing with that soft longing and with the feeling that you don't quite know what you're doing. Just be your unadorned self. Let the music play itself, no matter how strange or tentative it may feel or sound. Simple and unexaggerated as it is, it won't sound dull. This is an energetic simplicity—alive, pulsing, communicative.

As you continue playing or singing, you will sense a new intimacy with your instrument and the music. With the filters of the three styles removed, your body and heart feel more sensitive. You respond more readily to the delicate contours and harmonies of the music and bring them out naturally. You are struck by the depth of feeling that these musical shapes and colors convey.

Tape record your practicing, and compare this unaffected performance to previous ones in which you were engaged in various forms of struggle. Sometimes this simple approach gives the music a refreshing purity akin to a child's singing. Yet the performance also reveals the emotional depth of an adult.

You don't have to view this particular rendition of the music as an endpoint or a solution. Rather, it is a fresh start, a return to openheartedness from which you can work further. You can't measure how genuine you are or how close you are to playing or singing your best. But you can learn to trust this new performance as closer to the real you, emotionally bare, not trying to impress anyone, and not interfering with the natural flow of the music.

In any activity, hanging out with uncertainty teaches us confidence. You might walk into a party where you don't know anyone and you don't know exactly what to do. You don't have to rush to do anything. You can just notice how you feel, notice the room, the people, and the atmosphere, and be yourself, even if you feel awkward.

I remember experiencing such uncertainty when I was a beginner at meditation and I was invited to a small gathering after a talk at the meditation center. I walked into the room and found myself surrounded by people I didn't know who were talking about things I didn't understand. A wave of vulnerability and panic swept through me, and it must have showed in my face, because I suddenly noticed that a woman I had met a few minutes earlier was staring at me with great kindness. She obviously felt sympathy for me, and after chatting with her friends a few more minutes, she stood up, walked over to me, extended her hand, and said gently, "It was nice to meet you. Good night." Her soft voice and deep, kind eyes touched me, but I was too embarrassed to respond honestly. So I put on a big, false smile and said in a bright voice, "Good night!" Seeing that I wasn't ready to be more genuine, she was gone in a flash.

Years later, after I had been in her position many times

and had extended myself to others who looked shy and uncomfortable, I realized how magnetic my vulnerability must have been to her. In a world of artifice, such genuineness is refreshing.

In music as in life, we don't want to feel the embarrassment of being ordinary, foolish people. We want to soar to the heights making music and pretend we don't have clay feet weighing us down. Ironically, when we drop our guard and are just ourselves, we reveal a deep humanness and gentleness that connect us to humanity, and the music we make is uplifting.

I heard a performance several years ago at Carnegie Hall that exemplified gentleness and simplicity. In the middle of a concert featuring Jean-Pierre Rampal as flute soloist and conductor, Rampal's accompanist, John Steele Ritter, played Bach's F minor harpsichord concerto. The second movement of this concerto is slow and spare, with deep emotion conveyed with few notes. From the beginning to the end of this movement, vast space extended between one note and the next. Time stopped, and the hall was so still you could almost hear the audience breathing. No one moved. The soloist himself hardly moved but simply played the notes that were written, one after the other, not hurrying the music along, not caught up in anticipating what notes followed the ones he was playing at the moment, not trying to impress the audience or even to express himself in any special way. He just played, gently and unaffectedly, and the atmosphere was electric. The hall itself, with its sweeping curves of gold-embellished cream-colored walls and red velvet seats and railings, seemed to come alive and reverberate with the message "This is the high art for which this magnificent place was designed."

Being gentle does not mean that you play only soft, lyrical music. It means that you are willing to abandon inflated approaches and open yourself to the exact texture of music so that it penetrates you completely. The volcanic energy of Beethoven can flow through you freely, expanding to its full power because you do not try to manipulate it in any way. When you are unaffected and open to such wild energy, it reaches places in you that you didn't know existed, sparking your own energy in new ways. You thus meet your own mind as an artist and can begin to have genuine communication with an audience.

Some music is like a river, and you must let the currents flow through you. And some music is more like a raging fire. How do you accommodate a blaze in your body and mind? Relax and allow yourself to feel the heat. Just as a romantic look from across the room can create more passion than a hasty embrace, the most fiery music becomes even more intense when its flames have plenty of space in which to leap and dance. If you don't try to control fiery, forceful music, the roaring, crashing sounds take on a fullness and richness that only increase their power.

Can you be gentle with music that is diabolical, like Liszt's *Mephisto Waltz,* or primitive, like Stravinsky's *Rite of Spring?* The point is to be gentle with *yourself.* Allow yourself the luxury of not forcing yourself to re-create these energies. Feel your own body and mind as they are, sitting or standing with your instrument, letting the music pound through, letting yourself respond to it, and not knowing what will come out. Once you are relaxed and your energy is liberated from artificial controls, you can create a hair-raising performance. You just have to give up familiar strategies and leap into the unknown.

The vast, fresh space of the unknown may feel strange, but you can gradually become accustomed to the feeling of not knowing exactly what's happening or what will happen next. In this alternative approach—not indulging in passion, or treating the music casually, or attacking it—you discover a naked intimacy with the music, in which you also become intimate with yourself. As you get used to being so exposed, you begin to recognize that this feeling of not knowing is really the experience of meeting your naked self, and your shakiness can gradually develop into an unshakable conviction in your ability to communicate openly and directly.

To illustrate this paradoxical logic, let's go back to the examples in the previous chapter of meeting a person for the first time. Instead of struggling to express yourself to her, or to avoid her, or to control the situation, you can simply look directly at her, feel your heart beating, smile, and say, "It's nice to meet you." Your directness will probably be disarming.

Similarly, instead of grabbing the keys or the mouthpiece of your instrument with excessive passion or aggression, or lazily going through the motions, you can feel the unsureness of your touch and the fear and excitement of not knowing what will come out, and let it be brand new, like you're playing it for the first time.

Whether you are speaking or making music, communication requires that *you* say something. If you cloak yourself in emotional struggles and disguises, there is no real "you" to communicate; you don't come through. Think of a moment when someone revealed his vulnerable self to you through a shy glance, a quivering voice, a halting gesture, or a warm and touching musical phrase. We cherish such moments, for they express the humanness within us. Remember this the next time you find yourself perching uncertainly on the edge of the unknown. Trust yourself, and dare to express yourself genuinely.

CHAPTER 10

Pure Perception

Step Eight: Apply three listening techniques.

One day in a practice room at Indiana University I suddenly became curious: Could I apply the skill I'd acquired in ear-training class to the piano music I was learning? I tried to sing the bass line of a Bach partita while playing the right hand. I found I could sing only about half the notes in the bass line. I couldn't sing the rest because I couldn't hear them, even though I had been playing them for weeks. I spent the next several practice sessions singing all the lines in the piece until I could hear every note Bach wrote. A shockingly clear and vibrant performance came out of the piano; I was hearing the piece whole for the first time.

Incomplete hearing happens frequently. Sometimes, as with my Bach partita, we fail to hear the pitches we're producing. More often, we don't allow time for each sound to affect us completely. We are so busy humming the music in our mind and trying to control the instrument and the sound that we miss the moment of the music.

Receptiveness to music goes further than being able to tell the difference between C and D. You not only recognize different pitches and key changes but you receive their full impact and respond to them with your whole being. Your mind does not wander from the sound but is thoroughly engaged with it. You don't struggle with what you hear; you are simply filled with sound. You feel no separation between yourself and the sound.

Instead of fully experiencing sound, we often gloss over notes and struggle to manipulate a phrase to fit our preconceived idea of it. We try emphasizing different notes and adding crescendos, decrescendos, and subtle fluctuations of rhythm and tempo, but it never feels right. No matter how much we try, we can't make the music fall into place and lie flat because we have unwittingly stretched it out of shape. No matter how interesting our intellectual conception of a piece may be, it cannot be convincing if we do not completely hear the sounds.

Our hearing is innately acute. When we are relaxed and not rushing to go anywhere and when our mind is not cluttered, we notice sounds easily. We have room to take them in. But we often overload our sensory system and try to take things in at an impossible rate. We rush through learning a piece of music as though neither our perceptions nor the music were precious.

Vivid hearing is possible in each moment of practicing. You can consciously tune into sounds and let them touch you. This is *Step Eight: Apply three listening techniques.*

First Technique: Sing the notes and lines.

The first technique, which is for instrumentalists, is to sing every note and line in a piece. The voice was the first musical instrument, and because it is part of the body, we connect more naturally to music by singing than by playing an instrument. Also, when we sing, the vibrations of the voice massage the inside of the body. This sensation adds energy and vibrancy to the music we make.

I once taught at a music school where the faculty was required to conduct semiannual jury exams to evaluate students' progress. Although the piano teachers generally listened only to piano students, occasionally a voice student performed for us in these exams. I was struck by the emotional power of the singers as compared to the pianists, regardless of their level of technical accomplishment. Even the most amateur singers performed with a genuineness that went straight to the heart.

Singers and string players have to hear a note in their mind's ear before they can produce it with their instrument, so they are used to listening attentively. Pianists and guitarists, however, can just use their eyes to find the right keys or frets. It is easy for us to lose the vital connection between hand and ear. Singing revitalizes that connection.

String and wind players can also benefit from singing their music: It helps them hear it more clearly, so they can play more in tune. Violinist Frances Magnes points out that when every note is perfectly in tune, all the overtones come through, creating a vibrant sound. But when notes are slightly out of tune, overtones are missing and the sound lacks life.

Instrumentalists love to sing melodies from their pieces. As soon as the throat opens, we feel liberated from the limitations of habitual movements with our instruments. Singers, however, sometimes get caught up in the pursuit of vocal technique and lose touch with the fundamental purity of the voice. They, too, need ways of hearing music afresh. The listening techniques discussed later will address this need.

Instrumentalists such as pianists and guitarists who sometimes play more than one note at a time can benefit a great deal from the method I tried with my Bach partita—singing one line while playing others that occur simultaneously. This is like being in a chorus or an instrumental ensemble. You focus on your one line of notes, but you are also aware of the larger sound around you. Playing or singing one part in a large work is invigorating. Such invigoration infuses your practicing when you truly listen.

To try this technique, select one or two bars of a piece you have been studying. You can begin by singing the bass line while playing one or more other parts. Even chordal textures can be taken apart by singing lower, middle, or upper notes while playing the others. It is best not to hum. Take an upright posture and sing with your mouth open so that your body is fully engaged. Use either solfège syllables, if you are comfortable with them, or simply the syllable "la." After you have tried one combination of lines, switch to a different one; sing an upper line instead of the bottom one, for instance. Even if you can easily hear the upper melodic line of a phrase, you might be surprised what you notice when you sing it while playing other parts.

After you have taken apart one or two bars this way, play the section again, listening as you play. You will discover an astonishing difference in how you hear, move, and feel. Because you have opened your ears and taken all the sounds into your system, they fall into a natural order in your mind, and the phrase you were struggling to shape suddenly becomes simple and clear. In addition, once your perception is accurate, the brain transmits a clearer signal to the playing muscles so that your hands become better coordinated. Playing feels comfortable and light, both physically and mentally; the heaviness of your struggle is gone. It is shocking to first experience this effortlessness.

My student Lisa described this technique as a "magic key." The magic key is simply our own hearing, a capacity we always have but don't fully use.

I once suggested to a professional musician who was

preparing for an important solo recital that she practice her entire program by singing the parts this way. Although she admitted this technique had fantastic results, she said to me, "Who has time to practice that way?" It's true that the sheer number of notes in a composition, especially piano music, can be overwhelming. But we are responsible for these notes; our primary task as musicians is to hear what is written. Although this technique is difficult when you first try it, it gets easier with practice. If you are resistant to it, remember that these notes are not just a burden; they are a gift from a composer who put his whole being into writing them. If you take time to listen to each note, one by one they will connect to form the rich tapestry the composer created.

You can also sing lines in practicing chamber music. If you are a pianist, string player, guitarist, or percussionist, you can sing someone else's part while playing your own. It gives you a panoramic perception of musical events, and it brings the music to life.

Second Technique: Place your attention on the vibrations.

The second listening technique is to place your attention on the musical vibrations as they move through your body. This technique is for all musicians. It connects you to the physical reality of music.

Music is vibrations. When we listen to music, we experience the power of these vibrations. We are all familiar with the strong emotions that music elicits in us and how it can dissolve our preoccupation with problems or petty concerns. Yet strangely enough, such preoccupation also occurs when we practice. Either our mind wanders off the music, or we get caught up in musical concepts that obstruct direct experience of sound.

Sound is produced by movement and is itself movement. When a musician moves her body to play an instrument, the instrument responds by moving also. The sound that results is a continuation of that movement—vibrations are literally waves that move through the air. These waves in turn affect the substances in our bodies, including bones, membranes, and a variety of bodily fluids. So when we say we are "moved" by a piece of music, we are describing our experience in a literal way.

For the musician who produces the sound, this experience of creating and receiving vibrations is circular. The sound you make comes directly back to you. When you focus on the vibrations going through you, you experience music more viscerally. Simply play or sing a single note or chord of a musical phrase, and then take a moment to notice the effect it has on your body before you play or sing the next one. You may need to go extremely slowly at first—perhaps one note every one or two seconds—as you work against the habit of glossing over notes. But in contrast to much of the slow practice musicians do, this process is a pleasure. You discover a new level of sensation as you absorb pure sound, beyond your concepts about how it should be played or sung.

Once you become accustomed to listening this way, you can pick up speed without losing this vivid sensation of sound entering your system. Try to feel the vibrations going all the way down to your feet. You will find that just giving them your attention allows them to expand and to move more freely than before. You become saturated with them, achieving direct contact with the living texture of music. The mind of the composer lives in your body.

Hearing does not stop inside your ears; it takes place in the whole body. Even deaf people can dance to music because they feel the vibrations in their bodies. Musicians sometimes find that when they try to notice vibrations, their sensation stops at some point—at the level of their heart or stomach, for instance. If you notice that your feeling is blocked in one area, take extra time to focus on that area. Consciously let your breath enter the area for a minute or so. Then place your attention on the musical vibrations going into that place.

In working with an obstructed part of your body, notice if you have any mental or emotional associations with it. Consciously examining such obstacles often sheds enough light to dissolve them. A harpist who played for me found that she couldn't feel musical vibrations in her arms below the first few inches of her upper arms. I asked her to sit without her harp, open her arms, and notice how she felt. "Vulnerable and scared," came the reply. After staying with that feeling for a minute or two, she felt warmth spreading from her heart into her arms. When she played again the contrast was remarkable. She felt a rush of sensation in her arms, and her playing was richer and more energized than before.

Third Technique: Place your attention on each sound as it resonates in the space around you.

Music exists in space. In the previous technique we focused on the space inside the body. In this next technique we focus on the space outside the body.

This technique can be easier to apply than the other listening techniques. Play or sing the first note or chord of a phrase. Take time to notice how it affects you emotionally before playing or singing the next one. As with the previous technique, you may find you need to go very slowly. You will also find that the sound is more vivid than before. Within a short time you can pick up speed while maintaining keen awareness of the sound.

Try focusing on where the sound leaves the instrument and enters the air. If you are a singer, you can notice how the sound leaves your mouth and fills the room. Pianists, guitarists, and string players can focus on sonorities rising from the strings. Brass and woodwind players can notice how tones emanate from the ends of their instruments. Percussionists can notice the sound coming from its striking point.

Appreciate the unique sound of your particular instrument, and notice the precise texture of each individual sonority. The rich, raw sound of a bow rubbing against the strings of a cello is completely different from the luminous, ringing sound of a piano. As you move from one register to another, feel the change in quality. Let it affect you completely.

Let go of any judgments of the sound. Simply notice its quality. Singers in particular may be accustomed to listening critically to their sound. Voice teacher Jeannette Lovetri says that when a singer forgets about judging her results, she frees herself to focus more on the process. Then, even if some unpleasant sounds come out during the learning process, the end result may be a more beautiful sound, because it comes from deep within.

Each musical sound is unique. Three notes played with full attention contain more music than an entire piece played without it. A flutist played a short phrase in one of my workshops using this technique, and everyone present commented on how gorgeous it sounded. It was a revelation to the young man who played. "I'm hearing it," he said. "I haven't heard the music I've played for ten years."

While a teacher can help you learn when a particular listening technique is useful, you can accomplish a great deal simply by following your curiosity. Try these techniques and experience the results. Once you get used to them you will naturally be inclined to continue practicing this way. Tape recording your practicing provides helpful feedback on your progress.

These techniques allow you to perceive one sound at a time and respond to it with spontaneous ideas about how and when to produce the next sound. The following chapter will explore approaches to organizing music into groups, phrases, and textures.

Questions and Answers

Question: *Maybe instead of practicing as slowly as you suggest, we should practice at the tempo in which everything will be under control, every line, every note. It might not be so slow, but everything would be controlled. Isn't this more important?*

Answer: The word "control" is tricky. People often think of control as something artificial: "I am going to control this piece." What I'm describing is not control so much as a sense of natural command; you are totally connected to the music, and you have nothing to control because it's part of you. So you have complete confidence.

Sometimes we think, "I can play these notes; this feels comfortable," but we don't completely hear what we're doing. The performance comes out with all the notes intact, and it doesn't sound particularly tense, but it lacks emotional power. We could say we have good control, but we have not made a full connection to the music. Sometimes we have to slow down a lot in order to open ourselves up and make that full connection.

I read an interesting account by the pianist and composer Abram Chasins of how Rachmaninoff practiced. Chasins was approaching the house where Rachmaninoff was practicing and heard the legendary pianist playing so slowly that he couldn't tell what the piece was. He stood outside the front door for quite a while and finally realized it was the Chopin étude in double thirds, which is supposed to go like the wind. He timed the music on his watch and found that Rachmaninoff was playing one bar every twenty seconds—a little more than one note per second. We don't know why Rachmaninoff was practicing so slowly. But it's interesting that such a great virtuoso took so much time with each note.

Question: *When you're practicing slowly this way, feeling the vibrations, when does it get back up to tempo?*
Answer: You can trust your intuition about that. If you get tired of going slowly you can stop and try a different speed. These listening techniques are not meant to be practiced ad nauseam—especially singing lines. Playing one line and singing another is very difficult, and you wouldn't want to do it for a long time. But once your mind is connected to your ear, you can maintain the connection while speeding up.

Question: *How can you practice singing the notes if you don't have a very good ear and you can't hear them easily?*
Answer: People are born with different abilities, but you can develop your ear a lot. I had a student who couldn't sing back middle C when I played it. I had him practice it over and over, and then I asked him to sing the notes in his pieces as well. He got to the point where he could sing the left hand of Chopin's "Revolutionary" étude—an extremely fast and wide-ranging part—while playing the right hand.

Question: *If you sing one part and play another, and it's a very involved piece, like a Liszt étude, with thousands of notes all over the place, how do you cope with that? Do you recommend this technique for something like that, too?*
Answer: Yes. Sometimes a piece must eventually go faster than your voice can go. But it shouldn't go faster than you can hear it. So sing it until your voice can't go any faster, and then, as you play faster than that, pay attention to be sure you are hearing each note just as clearly as when you sang it. You may be surprised how much you can do.

Q: *If you are singing "La Campanella," for instance, and you have to do the leaps, which are totally out of your range, how would you do that?*

A: Transpose the octaves; sing the notes in whatever octave your voice can handle. This brings up an interesting point, which is that composers sometimes write a succession of notes that are intended to be heard as a texture of two or more layers. Sometimes the notes cover a wide pitch range, and sometimes they don't. But you find lines within lines, or lines within textures.

An Alberti bass is a simple example of this idea. You have a succession of sixteenth notes outlining a broken chord, arranged in groups of four, accompanying a melody. You don't necessarily have to sing all the notes in succession. You could instead break down the left-hand part into the actual bass line, which would consist of the notes that fall on the beats, and the three-note groups in between the beats. The ear tends to hear it as two parts instead of one, and if you sing it that way, you hear it more clearly. You start to notice how the piece was put together.

Question: *How do you separate out notes and sing them when the music is full of chords?*

Answer: When I feel as though I'm trying too hard to make sense out of music, I start to listen for individual notes. You can take a five-note chord apart. Don't play a whole section, but isolate the chord and see if you can sing one note while you play the other four. It doesn't take that much time, and it makes it easier to play that chord. Your fingers feel more independent; each one is connected to your brain because you're hearing the notes clearly, so each finger acquires special sensitivity. Don't be afraid to take things apart, no matter how complicated they are.

Question: *My problem with slow practice is that my mind wanders. I think I would really like to practice slowly this new way— if this exciting feeling of the sound vibrating will last a full minute before I start thinking about my grocery list. Could you say more about it?*

Answer: It's a practice, and you can develop it. The more you get into it the more it becomes a habit, and you don't want to work any other way.

Q: *Okay. So I'm going to play an A-flat chord, and I'm going to think about vibrations going through my shoulders and all around. But how long can that last? For me, it won't last very long. I'll start thinking about something out on the street.*

A: That doesn't matter. Everybody's mind wanders. The point is that when you notice your mind is wandering, you can bring it back to what you're doing by focusing on the sound.

We habitually hit ourselves over the head whenever we do something we don't feel good about. So if your mind wanders, you might think, "Oh, I'm terrible. My mind wandered." That's another habit; that's just another thought that you can let go of by bringing your attention back to the sound.

Also, the idea isn't to *think* about the sound going through. You just notice it. Place your attention on the vibrations, the feelings. It's quite different, very simple.

CHAPTER 11

Spontaneous Insight

Step Nine: Organize notes into groups, phrases, and textures.

For my eighteenth birthday, my parents sent me a tape recorder so I could become more aware of how my playing sounded and begin to be my own teacher. This was in the days before cassette recorders, and I was excited to receive this mini–reel-to-reel model that I could take with me to the practice room. The machine arrived with a tape of various members of the family playing music and speaking in honor of my birthday. My father played the piano, my sister played the flute, and the dog barked, prompted off the air by someone ringing the doorbell. One part of the tape stands out in my memory: my grandfather reading passionately in his Russian accent from the novel *Doctor Zhivago* about the nature of art. "Art comes from life," he read. "It is organic." The words left a deep impression on me and still move me today.

The life in a musical performance comes through in the natural ebb and flow of its phrasing, a rhythmic elasticity inherent in human pulse, breath, and movement. Unlike the rigid rhythms of machines, the rhythms we create and respond to most readily are flexible, like those we experience in our everyday activities—speaking, gesturing, walking, running, dancing, making love. And the music we make has a bodily logic that supports whatever intellectual logic we may find in it.

In order to discover the organic unity of a composition we must sense the rhythmic energy and direction of each small group of notes. We must be able to articulate the musical lines and textures we see on the page, to discriminate between which notes tend to flow forward and which tend to ebb, which notes require emphasis and which belong in the background. As one phrase after another takes shape and comes to life, together they accumulate into a piece of music. This is the work of *Step Nine: Organize notes into groups, phrases, and textures.*

The study of musical patterns and forms occupies a musician's lifetime and goes beyond the scope of this book. This chapter will explore the nature of musical rhythm and offer simple approaches to achieving rhythmic clarity and vitality and a sense of structural coherence.

Speech Rhythm and Body Rhythm

The music we hear today evolved from singing and dancing, and the rhythms of these two activities may be called "speech rhythm" and "body rhythm." Speech tends to follow the fluid, variable rhythms of breathing, while many bodily movements, such as walking or dancing, follow a regular pulse, like a heartbeat. But speech and song often contain the regular patterns characteristic of body rhythm. And bodily gestures often have the more lyrical, flowing rhythms of speech. So we find both kinds of rhythm in music, in endlessly varied combinations. A simple example is a waltz, which typically has both an "oom-pah-pah" type of accompaniment that establishes the pulse and a lilting melodic line that soars above it.

Balancing these two contrasting elements is an art. If a

robot were programmed to dance the waltz, it could go through the steps and keep time, but it would lack the heart and the flesh-and-blood body that give the movements grace and life. To make music or to dance with rhythmic vitality, you must let go joyfully and let yourself experience the living quality of the form.

My husband and I were once invited to a ball featuring Viennese waltzing, accompanied by the glorious music of Johann Strauss. In preparation, we took Viennese waltz lessons. Our teacher was very patient as we stumbled through the steps and tried to develop the elegant, uplifted quality of this dance. The day finally came when we stopped going through the motions and started waltzing. We felt an embarrassed excitement as our form became fluid and our bodies began to express the spirit of the music.

In learning a piece of music, we need to identify with its rhythmic form and spirit in a similar way. Counting out the beats will not suffice. Standing up without our instrument and singing and moving to the music can take us much further because it gets us physically involved with the lyrical and rhythmic energies in the piece.

Natural Rhythm

A great sense of rhythm comes from a body that feels free to move. Some cultures, such as the Caribbean, encourage a more relaxed relationship with the body than others. And some, such as the Italian, encourage more expressive use of the body. How we are brought up affects our rhythmic style and energy.

When my nephew was a few months old, my parents traveled to New York to see him. It was December, and one day during their visit, the baby, dressed in a bulky winter outfit, was lying on his back on the bed, fitfully thrusting his arms and legs in the air. My mother immediately understood what he wanted. "Get some of those clothes off him so he can kick around," she said. As soon as the sweaters and overalls came off, little Jonathan began kicking like mad, evidently having a great time. I was impressed with my mother's wisdom. I realized she must have encouraged the same freedom of movement in me when I was a baby, and that I owe some of my rhythmic vitality to her.

Developing Your Natural Sense of Rhythm

Whatever your cultural or family background is, you can develop your rhythmic sense by getting physical with the rhythms in music. Speaking through a phrase in rhythm, using syllables like "da dee daa," and overemphasizing the accented notes will clarify the rhythm in your mind. If you're studying vocal music, isolating the rhythm from the tune by speaking the words of the song in rhythm will clarify the phrasing. Opera conductor Adam Rosenbloom recommends comparing the notated rhythm with your normal speech rhythm in reciting the text in order to understand the composer's intention in bringing out certain words or images.

Making simple movements to mark the beats, such as swinging your arms back and forth or walking across the room, while singing or speaking a phrase will reinforce the musical pulse in your body. Improvising a dance to the music will encourage rhythmic freedom and expressiveness.

Some pieces are stylized dances with titles such as "Minuet" or "Polonaise." Learning the basic steps and character of these dances will allow you to play them in character. It's essential to know, for instance, that the second beat of the measure in a saraband is often slightly delayed, according to how it was danced centuries ago. The books *Dance of Court and Theater* by Wendy Hilton and *Dance and the Music of J. S. Bach* by

Meredith Little and Natalie Jenne provide a wealth of information about traditional dance patterns and structures. *Dance Pageant,* by Wendy Hilton and Donald Waxman, gives simple descriptions of each baroque dance and is a particularly useful resource for musicians. Some dance teachers occasionally offer classes in baroque dancing (see Resources for Musicians).

Moving rhythmically to music usually comes naturally to children. My first piano teacher sometimes had me skip around the room to music she played on the piano so that my body would learn the rhythm. Both children and adults can strengthen their rhythmic sense by taking a class in eurhythmics—a systematic approach to rhythm and movement that trains the student to feel and articulate musical rhythms with the whole body (see Resources for Musicians to locate a teacher).

Certain movement teachers and movement therapists are trained in "developmental movement"—the study of how we develop coordination from infancy onward, and how we can fine-tune our coordination by mastering early movement patterns that may not have fully developed. If you are interested in exploring your coordination from this point of view, working with a practitioner of Body-Mind Centering, the Feldenkrais Method, or Bartenieff Fundamentals can help free your body from old restrictive patterns (see Resources for Musicians).

ORGANIZATIONAL PRINCIPLES

Each musical phrase has a unique shape yet is organized according to universal structural principles. The Japanese use the term *jo ha kyu* to describe a structural principle that governs music, dance, drama, and all life events. *Jo* means

182

"orderly beginning." *Ha* means "breaking," "splitting off," or "scattering" from that beginning place—a gradual increase in complexity, density, and tempo. And *kyu* means "rapid conclusion." This particular Eastern organizational sensibility parallels the Western concept of beginning, building to a climax, and ending.

Entire concert programs are typically structured according to this principle. The opening work often has the quality of a gentle introduction, like an overture or a Bach prelude and fugue (*jo*). In the middle of the program, the music branches out to include a variety of moods and dramatic events (*ha*). Finally, we are likely to be treated to a rousing conclusion (*kyu*) that sends us home in an energetic state. The point of *jo ha kyu* is to create momentum, the sense of forward movement that gives an event a vital and satisfying quality.

This natural order occurs on every level of musical organization, from concert programs to individual phrases and groups of notes.[1] The rest of this chapter will discuss how to organize the mass of notes that comprise a musical work into groups, phrases, and textures that have momentum. In particular, I will focus on musical punctuation—identifying a natural beginning, middle, and endpoint for each group and phrase so that these small structural units connect coherently to form a living whole. Some musicians are more inclined than others to study the broad architecture of a piece when first learning it. But for all of us, the manual labor of mastering small groups of notes demands a great deal of time and attention. If we apply a few basic principles to articulating individual phrases and textures, the organic form of a work will gradually unfold.

The musical examples in the remaining sections vary in complexity. If you are a beginning student, don't worry if you can't understand each example in depth. Just absorb what you can and focus on the principles illustrated. Your understanding will suffice for your level of study and will develop as you study further.

Creating a Sense of Pulse: Grouping Notes "Over the Beat"

When I was a graduate student at the San Francisco Conservatory of Music, I took a class in Performance Practice. One day, the teacher played two recordings for us of the same orchestral work. The first performance emphasized every strong beat, which chopped up the music into small pieces and gave it a plodding quality. I felt relentlessly hit over the head by one beat after another. The second performance was just the opposite: It underplayed the strong beats, and the natural forward movement of the music lifted my spirits.

The following examples of grouping "Mary Had a Little Lamb" illustrate the difference between these two approaches. If you emphasize the beats and group the syllables in rhythm like this:

Ma - ry had a   lit - tle lamb,   lit - tle lamb,   lit - tle lamb

the verse sounds lifeless. But if you organize it this way:

Ma - ry had a   lit - tle lamb,   lit - tle lamb,   lit - tle lamb the phrase moves. In the first example, the beats, which are rhythmically strong points in the measure, receive too much emphasis. In the second, the beats are deemphasized, and the feeling of the offbeat moving toward the beat is strengthened, which creates a sense of momentum.

The mind cannot comprehend a long series of notes without dividing it into small segments. Even the seven digits of a telephone number are divided into a group of three digits followed by a group of four. Similarly, musical phrases strike the ear in groups of two, three, and four notes. But the visual impression we receive from a page of printed music is deceiving. If we try to hear the music in the groups we see—pausing after each group of four sixteenth notes connected by beams, for instance, or after each group of triplet eighths—the music usually falls apart into meaningless fragments:

Mozart: Piano Sonata in C Major, K. 545, 1st mvt.

But if we take the same music and divide the notes as follows:

each group makes sense to the ear. It is coherent and musical. In the second example, I have added a dash over the second note of each slurred group of four sixteenth notes (the third note of the printed group) to indicate that it has a slight emphasis: It functions as an offbeat note leading to the next beat, providing a sense of forward movement. This emphasis is not necessarily an increase in volume; it is more likely to occur as an imperceptible lengthening of the note.

Play or sing this section of the music with actual pauses between these units to clarify the grouping in your mind. Once the grouping is clear, go through the section without pauses but still hearing it organized this way. The music will come to life instead of coming to a halt on every beat. It will swing instead of sounding like a sewing machine.

Harpsichordist Ralph Kirkpatrick refers to this organizing principle as "the enchainment of impulses from active upbeats." [2] Although he refers specifically to "active upbeats" (faster moving notes that lead into a new measure), offbeat notes at other points in a measure can also initiate forward movement and help link groups of notes into an unbroken chain.

Some musicians habitually break the chain of forward movement by pausing before crucial notes in an effort to be expressive, instead of letting the music flow directly to those notes. If you hear this section of Chopin's B flat minor nocturne with obvious pauses, indicated by commas, as follows:

you diminish the impact of the harmonic changes and break the forward flow. Instead, you could hear it this way, with each comma indicating only the beginning of a new group and a barely perceptible delay of the first note of the group:

Now momentum has a chance to build and the music sustains your interest more.

This same principle applies to complete measures. In many cases, if you view barlines as dividing points, the music stops at each one. Try hearing this section of a Schubert waltz with commas at the barlines:

Schubert: Waltz in B Major, Op. 18, No. 2

If you try to dance to the music with this grouping, your foot feels too heavy on the downbeat and your body feels uncoordinated.

Now organize the music so that each unit ends just after the downbeat, as follows:

When you dance the waltz this way, feeling the count as

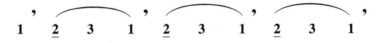

you feel a lift on each first beat and a sense of forward flow.

Great composers frequently imply such grouping of notes by placing rests on the downbeats. Edward E. Lowinsky's essay "On Mozart's Rhythm" makes a comparison between two themes from piano sonatas by Mozart and Johann Christian Bach. The melodic and harmonic material of both themes is similar, but Mozart's theme has more life partly because the accompaniment has rests on the downbeats.[3]

J.C. Bach: Sonata in G, Op. V, No. 3, 1st mvt.

188

Mozart: Sonata in B flat, K.333, 1st mvt.

Once you are aware of the basic principle of grouping notes over the beat and over the barline, look for exceptions to this rule. Sometimes a downbeat, instead of an upbeat, initiates a new group or phrase. And sometimes the last note of a group functions as a "dovetail"—it also begins the next group. Music is infinitely rich and complex, and several different approaches to the same section can each make sense in different ways and contribute to your understanding of the music. By experimenting with a variety of approaches to a piece, you will develop your musical intelligence, and a coherent performance will evolve.

Impulses and Riding the Energy from Impulses

When we speak, we emphasize specific words or syllables to give meaning to a sentence. By changing the emphasis from one word to another, we alter the meaning. For example, the sentence "I'm going to the store" might be spoken with the accents on the second and last words as follows: "I'm *going* to the *store.*" This choice of emphasis clarifies that the action is "going" (as opposed to staying or leaving) and the destination is the "store" (as opposed to the library, the park, or a party). But we might instead choose to emphasize the first word: "*I'm* going to the store." In this case, the speaker is clarifying that *he,* not someone else, is going to the store. We make such distinctions automatically, based on our intentions and emotions as we speak.

Music is the same. Even in instrumental music, which does not have words, our familiarity with the language of music gives us a sense of which notes in a phrase require emphasis. As in speech, we create that emphasis by making a louder sound, or by pausing minutely before a sound, or by both of these methods.

Take the following sentence: "I told you I didn't want you to do that ever again." Spoken quietly, some syllables would naturally sound louder than others: "I *told* you I *did*n't want you to *do* that *ev*er a*gain*." If you want to make your statement more emphatic, however, you might pause slightly before the word "ever" and accent its first syllable more strongly: "I *told* you I *did*n't want you to *do* that '*EV*er again." And you can make it still more emphatic by adding a pause before the last word and strengthening its accent: "I *told* you I *did*n't want you to *do* that '*EV*er 'a*GAIN* !"

The energy from a strong impulse on a single syllable will carry the voice through several syllables following it. In the examples in the above paragraph, the italicized syllables *"told," "did," "do,"* and *"EV"* are spoken with renewed energy that continues over the unemphasized syllables that follow.

The following phrase from the last movement of Mozart's Piano Concerto in A Major, K. 488, illustrates this principle of "riding the energy" from an impulse:

In this example, the main emphasis is on the high A on the first beat of the second measure: I have added a dash over the note to indicate more volume, and a comma before the note to indicate a slight delay, as if you are taking a breath. Because of this emphasis, the high A sounds jubilant, and both your hand and the music have enough energy to carry them through to the end of the phrase with ease and élan. But if you place the primary accent on the first note of the first measure instead, you begin to run out of steam in the middle of the run:

"Taking a breath" before the high A does not contradict the principle of grouping the left-hand eighth notes over the beat. If you hear these notes as leading forward to the downbeat of the second measure, the music will have momentum and buoyancy regardless of the comma before the high A.

When you're riding the energy of an impulse and approaching the end of the phrase, keep riding instead of dragging out the ending. The habit of slowing down considerably at the end of phrase after phrase gives the effect of constantly letting the air out of a performance so that it falls flat. It's more exciting to keep moving and to use dynamics (changes between loud and soft) and only subtle changes of tempo to shape most phrases. In a convincing rubato, each phrase builds from its beginning and runs its course naturally, like an exhalation, so that the next one may begin without a loss of momentum.

Sometimes the opposite habit occurs: We don't let the exhalation happen. We try to initiate a new phrase when we haven't let the previous one taper off and die. This is like trying to inhale before you've finished exhaling. It creates tension that needs to be released. Practice playing or singing through to the end of a phrase without anticipating the next one. By keeping your attention on the present moment, you will discover more subtleties in the music, and it will flow more naturally.

By experimenting with the dynamics in a phrase, you can round out the basic shape created by the placement of emphases and cast the same phrase in different lights. It frequently feels natural to increase the volume when the pitch rises and to decrease it when the pitch descends. The Mozart example on page 191 works well if you apply this concept. But the wealth of harmonic and rhythmic changes in music requires infinite variations on this approach.

This book cannot begin to explore the vast and important subject of harmonic and tonal analysis, but by applying the listening techniques described in the previous chapter along with these principles of grouping and phrasing, you can gradually develop an intuitive understanding of the harmonic and tonal structure of a composition. If you would like to sharpen your intellectual understanding as well, I recommend studying Heinrich Schenker's brilliant method of tonal analysis. The two-volume set of books titled *Structural Hearing: Tonal Coherence in Music* by Felix Salzer explores Schenkerian analysis in depth. *Harmony and Voice Leading* by Edward Aldwell and Carl Schachter lays an excellent foundation for studying Schenker's approach.

Articulating a Texture

The left-hand part of the Mozart example on page 191 is a series of four-note figures rather than a melodic line. This series functions as an accompanimental pattern or texture that complements and supports the right-hand melody. Because each figure is a broken triad, you can simplify the accompaniment by thinking of it as a succession of block chords, the bass notes of these chords connecting to form a bass line (A, G#, A, E). The upper notes also create a line (E, F#, E), as do the middle notes (C#, D, C#).

Hearing this accompaniment as a weave of vertical and linear elements gives the repetitive and potentially monotonous pattern a bubbling energy that suits the rollicking nature of the melody above it. Grouping the eighth notes over the beat helps to delineate the lines in the accompaniment by setting off each bass and upper note with a comma between them (remember that these commas indicate grouping, not obvious pauses):

The play of one part against another is richest in contrapuntal writing. Not only do faster notes in one melodic line flow simultaneously with slower ones in another, but accents and impulses appear in different voices at different times, creating a sense of rhythmic independence of the different parts. Singing one line of a keyboard composition while playing the others will help you not only to hear the pitches but to clarify the contrasting rhythms: You articulate one rhythm with your voice and the others with your hands.

Kirkpatrick's concept of "the enchainment of impulses from active upbeats" applies specifically to what he calls the "rhythmic influence" of one voice upon another. The opening of Bach's G major French suite is an excellent example of this principle:

At the end of each measure, one or more voices lead into the next measure with an active upbeat. When you clearly feel this leading quality, you continuously regenerate forward-moving energy. You also bring out the play of voices against one another, which enlivens the texture.

For all its romanticism and emotional volatility, the music of Chopin is meticulously notated to reveal a sophisticated polyphony that is often highly contrapuntal. The following excerpt is shown with two different sets of commas to indicate different approaches to grouping:

Chopin: Piano Concerto in F minor, 1st mvt.

Experimenting with different groupings can be a way of reveling in the sensuous mix of sounds in this passage. Grouping notes thoughtfully and bringing all the lines into focus by singing each one while playing others is essential in this complex music. If we do not reveal the rich detail in Chopin's writing, we take something away from its emotional substance. We risk reducing this intensely passionate music to mere fluff, weak sentimentality, or bombast. But if we bring out the syncopations and harmonic inflections, we enjoy a lyricism that has fiber, pungency, and sparkle.

Impressionist music is full of shimmering textures that evoke visual scenes and elemental forces in the world. Rain, clouds, and mist sparkle in varying degrees of sunlight. Magically, the music re-creates the scenes described by the titles: "Jardins sous la pluie" (Gardens in the Rain), "Une Barque sur L'Ocean" (A Boat on the Ocean), "La Cathédrale Engloutie" (The Sunken Cathedral), "Des Pas sur la Neige" (Footsteps in the Snow).

In the following passage from "Noctuelles" (Night Moths) by Ravel, the first phrase is a cascade of right-hand triplets against left-hand duplets, which form chord streams, with five notes in each chord:

Rather than trying to group these notes over the "beat," you can simply bring out the top line (the upper notes of the chords) and hear the other notes as a fluttering pattern, like moths fluttering as they descend in flight. Hearing the music in chordal units this way accentuates the play of fluctuating dissonant harmonies against a lyrical line, creating the effect of changing refractions of light.

The second phrase works well if you hear the first eight notes (starting on C) as a fluttering chromatic line leading to the high C, which moves down to B flat:

The eight ascending notes backtrack a half-step halfway through, effectively reinforcing the sense of upbeat, as well as perpetuating the image of beating wings. Hearing the ascending line as a long upbeat (or a double upbeat) keeps the music moving forward by rebuilding tension that has begun to dissolve in the previous phrase.

Emergence

Hearing music in coherent groups, phrases, and textures makes it easier to play or sing. Many musicians have had the experience of struggling to execute a particular passage and finding that once they organized the notes more intelligently, technical problems disappeared. Music flows more easily through the body when it flows more coherently in the mind.

As the sense of physical and musical flow develops with a piece, the music gradually comes to life within you and dictates more and more clearly what it needs to make it breathe, sing, and dance. Just as the technique of absorbing the psychological effect of each sound allows you to approach the next one sensitively, noticing the effect of each group, phrase, or texture will help you link it naturally to the one that follows, Each time you articulate one small element, you shed light on the work as a whole and reveal more of its brilliance.

In understanding the organic form of a composition, you become its co-creator, discovering its hidden facets, which you can illuminate for an audience. Trust your intelligence in exploring the myriad patterns and shapes in a piece of music. You can unlock the secrets that bring it to life.

CHAPTER 12

The Dancing Body

Step Ten: Place your attention on the sensations of touch and movement.

My first memory of playing the piano is of my father teaching me to play a tune from Mozart's opera *The Marriage of Figaro* when I was six years old. I had just begun lessons, and he used my teacher's system of writing numbers on the keys from one to eight, covering the C major scale. After writing the numbers for the melody on a piece of paper, he sang it with me and taught me to play it phrase by phrase. I felt the music jump out of my body through my fingers and into the piano with a power and sureness that thrilled me more than any other playing experience I can remember. For the first time, I had the vivid sensation of making music myself.

For all of us, the impulse to make music is to get our body into it, to use our hands, lips, voice, and breath to create music physically, sensually. But in the midst of our struggles to read the score, execute arpeggios, and shape phrases, we lose touch with the skin that touches the instrument and with the energy that flows through the body as we move. *Step Ten: Place your attention on the sensations of touch and movement* is designed to help you reconnect with your body and to increase the physical pleasure of making music. The more you enjoy using your body, the better your coordination and sound will be.

Imagine that you are blind. To learn to play your instrument you can't watch your teacher play; you must develop a keen awareness of exactly how your body moves and how the instrument feels against your skin or lips. With the visual world unavailable to you, the sensory world inside your body becomes extremely familiar. When you sing, you are intensely aware of the physical sensation of breathing and of using your voice.

Compare this image of a blind musician to a pianist who looks at the keyboard while he plays. Instead of knowing the moves thoroughly with his body, he relies on his vision to find the right keys. To execute a leap, he has to first look and then move, which complicates the process of playing and delays his hand's arrival at its destination. His fingers lack the sureness and familiarity with the instrument that the blind musician has. This vision-oriented player is like a dancer who relies on chalk marks on the floor to know where to step: He moves awkwardly instead of easily and fluidly. Smooth, confident movement can occur only if his whole body knows the steps, so that he is free to dance without keeping track of every spot his feet have to touch.

When I was eighteen, I tried playing the piano without looking at my hands. I made a few mistakes, but I was amazed by the increased sense of command and intimacy with the instrument and the music. With a little practice, I gained accuracy as well. Twenty years passed, however, before I tried this method again, after reading an article that advised it. This time, I was so amazed by the results that I continued working this way.

Other musicians have had similar experiences. Violist Karen Ritscher discovered a new sense of command when she began playing her instrument without watching her left hand move up and down the fingerboard. Like many players, she used to support the viola with her left shoulder so that her head faced the fingerboard. When she adopted the more comfortable habit of using her collarbone to support the instrument, her head faced forward, away from the fingerboard, and she could no longer see her hands so easily (see photos in Chapter 6, page 90). Since the instrument has no frets, watching the left hand doesn't serve much purpose. "If anything," Ms. Ritscher says, "it takes away from listening, because more energy gets tied up with keeping track of your fingers. So now I hear more, I'm more comfortable, and I enjoy playing more. I play much better this way."

If you are a string player, you may be accustomed to using a mirror to observe details of your technique—to make sure the bow is perpendicular to the strings, for instance, or that you are not dropping your right elbow. Some string teachers even videotape their students to show them how they are playing. While mirrors and video screens can be helpful, students sometimes become dependent on these visual aids, and their kinesthetic sense lags behind. To balance your practice habits, focus more on the sensations of touch and movement and use your vision mainly to check that what you feel is in accord with what you see.

Many wind players also use mirrors to check their posture and position, but they rely heavily on their kinesthetic sense as well. Flutist Janet Weiss says that the main purpose of practicing long tones is "to develop a sense of where each note is in the face and in the breathing column, and to learn what amount, speed, and angle of wind you need." The more in tune you are with sensations, the better your technique will be. A trombonist once asked me to help him with his playing. He had difficulty producing a clear sound, and I noticed he seemed to lack lip control. I asked him to consciously feel each note in his mouth before blowing. When he focused this way, he played with more ease and produced a much clearer sound.

Singers also need to feel notes in their mechanism before producing them. Voice teacher James Carson uses a method (described at the end of Chapter 6) in which you "think the sound" you want to produce and then notice how movement automatically occurs in the back of your throat as the vocal cords prepare to make the sound. "Think both the pitch and the vowel color beforehand," he advises, "and then discover the sensation your brain has created for you." While many singers attempt to produce the right vowels by deliberately changing the shape of their mouth, this mental approach to vowel formation actually brings a stronger sense of the exact physical movements required to produce the sound, which makes singing easier. Try this method by thinking the syllable "ee," then "oo," taking care not to deliberately shape the vowel. Notice how movement occurs in your throat and mouth in preparation for each vowel.

Singers often listen critically to the quality of their voice and get so caught up in struggling for a bigger and better sound that they lose touch with their bodies. One singer told me that at a certain point in her vocal study she "didn't dare trust any sensation she had" because she was so fixated on her sound. Then one of her teachers said to her, "Don't you like the way it feels? When I sing, it feels like I'm massaging my throat." Once she began noticing the sensations in her throat, she enjoyed singing more and produced a fuller, more beautiful sound.

Pianists and guitarists can improve their sound dramatically by practicing most of the time without looking at the keyboard or fretboard. If you're an arch beginner, you will naturally want to become familiar with what your hands do by watching them in action. But you can also tune into how they feel. Try playing a passage once looking at your hands, then play it "blind."

Mirta played for me for the first time at a workshop I conducted one evening at Steinway Hall in New York. She played a simple Chopin Mazurka quite musically, but when she tried it again without even glancing at the keyboard, the exquisite sound and phrasing that came out of the piano made the audience gasp.

David, a young professional guitarist, had a similar experience in a workshop at my studio. After giving a stiff, inexpressive performance of a work by Albéniz, he tried it again without looking at the frets to position his hands. His playing relaxed and came alive. Everyone in the group complimented him enthusiastically on his performance.

What explains these magical transformations? Focusing on sensations in your hands increases your awareness of their movements, which enables them to find their way around with more sensitivity and precision. As your fingers learn the exact location of every key, string, or fret, your arms follow your hands in their deft navigation of the instrument and draw your whole body into smooth, natural movement. This technical security and ease, along with the increased physical pleasure that comes with heightened awareness of sensation, allows music to flow more directly and spontaneously. Your unique personal energy comes through the music.

How to Focus on Sensations

Either closing your eyes or looking ahead of you will help you tune into sensations. I prefer keeping my eyes open because I like having an awareness of the environment and because the experience is similar to performing. But experiment and find out what works best for you. In either case, visualizing the keys, strings, fingerboard, or bow will help you gauge the distances your hands and arms need to travel. If you are a singer or wind player, you can visualize the breathing or vocal mechanism within your body.

Touch and movement are interrelated. According to a basic law of physics, when you touch an instrument, the body's force against the instrument creates an equal and opposite reaction: Energy flows back into the body from the instrument. Notice the play of forces within your body as you contact your instrument and as energy circulates through your system. Let yourself enjoy these sensations.

If you feel stiff, try focusing on the space inside your arms containing blood and other bodily fluids. Remembering that your arms are alive and not completely solid will allow you to release tension and express yourself more freely.

Accuracy

You are bound to make mistakes practicing this way, but you might be surprised how few notes you miss. The longer you have been using your instrument with good body mechanics, the more familiar your body will be with the complex movements it makes. Your body is intelligent. Relax and trust it. You will gradually acquire greater accuracy and technical security.

Some teachers advise note-perfect practicing in order to learn the precise right movements from the beginning. But as long as you depend on your eyes to play the right notes, your coordination cannot fully develop; your movements will not become as smooth, reliable, or powerful as they could be.

To develop accuracy, practice positioning your hand one note ahead of the note you're playing. For instance, if you're playing an ascending C major scale on the piano with your right hand, at the moment that you play E with your third finger, you should be moving your thumb to F. When you play F, your second finger should already be on G. You're always in position as you go along, so your movements are efficient and precise. Extremely stretched positions, however, create strain, so don't stretch your hand sooner than necessary to reach distant keys or strings.

Some passages pose special problems. In performance, your vision can help you find certain notes and maximize your chances for accuracy. And it is unnatural to constantly stare off into space or keep your eyes closed while an audience is watching. But during practice, the body must learn to negotiate the trickiest reaches by feel.

At her lesson one afternoon, Jennifer played a Scarlatti sonata in A major in which the right hand repeatedly crosses rapidly back and forth over the left. She kept miscalculating these jumps and missing notes, and she had never tried to play these sections without looking at her hands because she thought it was impossible. I asked her to visualize the keyboard in her mind and suggested that as her right hand bounced off each key, she should simultaneously aim in her mind for the next one. This simultaneous striking and aiming is like hitting a ball over a net: If you're aware of the direction you want the ball to go in, you can send it to the desired destination.

Jennifer summoned her powers of concentration but still made several mistakes. I then asked her to focus on the sensation of her sit bones rooting her to the bench, and on the slightly different sensation of each arm movement, from the shoulder blade to the tips of her fingers, as her hand made an arc in space. With these reference points of her sit bones and her shoulder blade, she developed a clear sense of exactly how far her hand was traveling from the center of her body to each key. Her performance suddenly became note-perfect.

At a later lesson, Jennifer played Brahms' Rhapsody, Opus 79, No. 2. She had practiced it without looking at the keyboard but was still having trouble with some of the octave jumps in the left hand, which appear in these opening bars:

She tried playing only the bottom notes of the octaves to become familiar with the distances her fifth finger needed to travel, but she couldn't get the big jump from the A below low A, on the last beat of the second measure, to the low C above it, on the first beat of the next measure. Then I suggested she focus on making the shift from the thumb on low A to the fifth finger on low C. This way, to make the octave jump of a tenth, she needed to focus only on a distance of a third. With this approach, the passage became manageable, and she played it accurately with ease.

Jennifer's accuracy in both of these passages, the Scarlatti and the Brahms, varied over the course of several weeks, mostly depending on how well she was able to focus on different days. But regardless of how many mistakes she made at times, she enjoyed the keen awareness of bodily sensations, she noticed her accuracy was generally improving, and she began to acquire a new, exciting sense of command of her body and the instrument. Her performance soon became powerful and reliable.

Notice How Your Body Wants to Move

One day in 1984, the pianist, composer, and teacher Eloise Ristad spent four hours in my apartment listening to me play and making unusual suggestions to free up my music-making energy. Among them was, "Notice how your hands want to move." The idea that my hands could have a mind of their own seemed strange, but as soon as I tried tuning into their whims, they began to move more freely and produced a more dynamic performance.

Try this yourself. Simply pay attention to whatever body parts are moving to produce sound from your instrument. Notice how your hands, arms, lips, or breathing muscles want to move, and let them move that way.

Notice particularly how each movement needs a sense of completion, or "follow-through." Follow-through is what happens when you hit a tennis ball: Your arm keeps moving after the ball leaves the racket. Similarly, when you play a note or phrase on the piano, the hand and arm often want to continue moving in some way after you strike the key(s). Let them keep moving naturally instead of freezing in any one position or limiting your range of movement.

You can also practice follow-through in daily activities, such as combing your hair or walking. I often notice when I walk down the street that I am not letting my body move freely. As soon as I pay attention to how my legs want to move, my walking becomes both more expansive and better coordinated. Simple movement becomes a pleasure.

Acting teacher George Morrison teaches a similar approach

called "moving for pleasure" at the New Actors Workshop in New York. His students cultivate natural movement for the stage by practicing one rhythmic, repetitive movement at a time and focusing on bodily sensations, until they can say, "This feels good, free, and light." They continue the movement until they can say, "This feels even better, even freer, and even lighter." Mr. Morrison is describing the increased pleasure we can all experience if we make a practice of noticing the sensations of moving our bodies.

The more you cultivate the habit of moving freely and pleasurably in nonmusical activities, the more it will carry over into practicing your instrument. When you let your body move freely, its full expressive range emerges. You discover more of who you are, you bring more of your own richness, power, and subtlety to the music you make, and you hear more of the music's beauty and depth in return.

So instead of forcing your body to control your instrument, tune into your sensations, trust your innate coordination and musicality, and let yourself move spontaneously. Let your body make the music. It has a brilliant mind of its own.

QUESTIONS AND ANSWERS

Question: *Sometimes I practice difficult passages on the piano with one hand at a time before trying to combine the hands. This is easier than using two hands, but when I put the hands together, the sensations are very different from what I feel with either hand alone, and I have to practice it longer to get used to it. Am I wasting my time playing with one hand? Should I practice "blind" with both hands all the time?*

Answer: Playing with both hands *is* like a third animal—coordinating the whole mechanism involves more than coordinating the sum of the parts. But using both hands sometimes takes more focusing ability than we have, especially when we're first learning a difficult passage.

Practicing is very much about focusing on one thing at a time and working gradually toward the experience of the whole. Even when you focus on the sensations of playing with both hands, those sensations are only one aspect of what is happening. A musical composition begins with one sound; you build your performance from that first sound and from your first perceptions of the piece. In this building process, you have the luxury of taking the music apart, becoming intimate with its details, and putting it back together with new insight. So if you want to get thoroughly acquainted with either hand individually in a particular passage, do it. Any experimenting you do with clear focus will improve your coordination, deepen your understanding of the piece, and strengthen you as a musician.

Question: *In your entire approach to practicing, and especially in this last step, I recognize that you're describing a feeling I've experienced of letting go. How do you keep that sensation of tuning in and listening and experiencing, yet still keep your alert intelligence that lets you know where you're going? How do you make sure that you repeat the section that you wanted to repeat, and that you remember the notes, and that everything works together, so that you have a watchfulness—so that you are still* there *in some form?*
Answer: Musicians are sometimes afraid that if their mind perks up they won't be able to trust it. It's similar to being afraid that if you take in everything that's around you, you won't know you should cross the street on a green light. You think you'll become some kind of zombie. The opposite is true. But you have to experience it in order to know.

What I'm describing is the kind of brilliant awareness that we typically experience only in rare situations as passive observers. For instance, you're walking down the street thinking about all kinds of things, when suddenly a car crashes right in front of you, and you become extremely aware of where you are. You're wide awake and not at all aware of what was distracting you before.

You don't have to depend on a dramatic event like a car accident to wake up. At any moment, if you deliberately place your attention on the details in front of you, you can stop the chatter in your mind. It's an active rather than a passive approach to receptivity.

Q: *So you use your mind to place your attention on the details, and you let go?*

A: Yes.

Q: *But how do you balance letting go and not letting go?*

A: Trust yourself and find out. In my experience, when I start to let go, I wake up much more than I thought I could. This is where the line between practicing and performing starts to dissolve, because when you're on the spot in a performance, your usual mental chatter diminishes and is overwhelmed by the brilliance of the moment. So you have to let go and trust yourself. If you practice letting go, you build a habit of trusting yourself and taking risks, so that performing is less terrifying.

PART THREE

Natural Command

CHAPTER 13

Playing by Heart

I once heard a famous pianist play Beethoven's Sonata in A Flat, Opus 110, in a recital at San Francisco's Masonic Auditorium. The hall was full, and I sat far from the stage in a crowd of three thousand people. He performed wonderfully, with the clarity and radiant sound I had always loved in his recordings. But halfway through the Fugue of this magnificent sonata, he suddenly stopped cold, paused, and began the movement again from the beginning. He had obviously had a memory lapse.

The critic wrote in the paper the next day that "it was a stroke of genius" that the artist chose to begin the Fugue again rather than try to find his way back on course in the middle of this complex movement. I asked myself, "If this fine pianist were not so famous, would the critic still have thought his starting over was a stroke of genius? Or would he have said, 'Unfortunately, Mr. So-and-So had such a disastrous memory slip in the middle of the Fugue that he had to start all over from the beginning'? If it had been me up there onstage, what would he have said?"

The possibility of having a memory lapse in public frightens us. Our doubts about our talent and our fears of being seen by others as inadequate performers frequently focus on this one issue. We tend to think, "If I were really talented and really deserved to be performing, I wouldn't be so afraid of playing from memory and my memory wouldn't fail me."

Two Types of Talent

The German language has two words for "musical." *Musikantisch* means physiologically musical—capable of hearing and thinking music. This type of musicality includes the ability to memorize easily, as well as other types of facility, such as good sight-reading and a sense of pitch—either perfect pitch or strong relative pitch. *Musikalisch,* on the other hand, refers to artistic musicality, the ability to make music with passion, intelligence, and sensitivity.

In his book *A Comprehensive Approach to the Piano,* Alexander Libermann tells two stories that illustrate these two different types of musicality. A twelve- or thirteen-year-old boy, who was considered a prodigy and who had performed extensively, came to play for Libermann. He found the boy's playing disappointingly dull and gave him some musical tests. First, he played a series of tone clusters, and the child identified each note in them. Then he asked him to sight-read and transpose Bach fugues, which he did with ease but without feeling or intelligence. Finally, Libermann tested the boy's memory, and found that after he read through a Beethoven sonata a few times, he had the piece memorized. Thinking that this boy *was* a genius who had simply not been well taught, he worked hard with him for a year but failed to uncover any artistic ability.

Ten years later, a middle-aged woman arrived at Libermann's studio in a desperate state and told him, "I don't even know why I came here. I'm a hopeless case; all that interests me in life is to play the piano, and I know that I will never be able to because I am not only unmusical, I am *a*musical." Libermann asked her to play, expecting very little. To his surprise, she gave one of the most beautiful performances he had ever heard—warm, sensitive, and intelligent. She played a second piece equally well, but when he asked for a third, she burst into tears. "That's the trouble," she said. "I *can't* play anything else. I took years and years to learn those two pieces." He taught her for a while, and although her technique improved a little, she wasn't able to learn music any faster than before.[1]

Over the course of his several decades of teaching, Libermann observed that every musician possesses these two types of musicality in different proportions. Some performers are "giants"—they have it all. Measuring ourselves by what the giants can do may help us decide how ambitious to be in our musical careers. But if we use this measurement to "prove" that we are musically untalented or unfit to perform, we hurt ourselves and needlessly undermine our confidence.

The Challenge of Memorization

Performing music from memory is a great feat. Doctors and scientists agree that making music, even during practice, stretches the human capacity for neuromuscular precision and emotional flexibility to the maximum. With the body, mind, and emotions functioning at this peak level, the added element of the adrenaline rush that occurs during concert performance can throw us off balance.

Sometimes we lose our place in the music because we aren't thoroughly prepared. But because many excellent performers also have memory lapses, we fear that no amount of preparation can guarantee perfect memory during our next concert or audition. Some musicians are so afraid of having a memory slip that they perform with the score. Yet, as many of us know, in the heat of performance, even with the printed page in front of us, we may suddenly find our fingers or our mouth moving off course, leaving us momentarily bewildered and interrupting the flow of the music.

Some memory lapses occur because we become self-conscious while performing. Instead of letting ourselves enjoy the intense energy running through us, the vitality of this wonderful moment, we worry about the next section we have to play, criticize ourselves for how we played the last section, or congratulate ourselves on how we are doing. Or we might suddenly think about a certain person in the audience and imagine he is not pleased with our performance. Any number of such thoughts can snag our minds, impeding a free musical outpouring.

The next chapter will discuss performance as a practice, in which we learn to let go of self-consciousness and allow the energy of the music, and of the fear and excitement of performing, to flow freely through our body and mind. But first let's look at memorization itself—the process of becoming conscious of music and movement in order to make the music a part of us.

If we focus less on ourselves, our doubts, and our fears, and instead lose ourselves in the joys of working with music and of becoming intimate with it, we encourage natural memorization. As children, we called this process "playing by heart"—a phrase that conveys both the feeling of knowing a piece intimately and the longing to possess deep knowledge of music, to make it a part of us, to be one with it.

Creating a Safety Net

When I was in my twenties and living in Berkeley, California, I had a date to play Beethoven's Third Piano Concerto with a local orchestra. As part of my preparation, I went to a pianist friend's house a couple of weeks before the concert and played the piece for him. It went well, but I told him I was anxious about being able to perform it from memory. The possibility of losing my place while the orchestra kept playing threw me into a panic. I said I had to make sure that my memory would be perfect in the performance, that nothing would go wrong.

As I looked up from the piano bench, I saw my friend striding toward me, shaking his head of curly red hair and gesticulating wildly, saying, "Is *that* what you think memorization is for? To make sure that nothing goes wrong? No! It's so that if something *does* go wrong, you'll know the music well enough to find your way out of the problem."

He spoke wisely. In the performance, my left hand got lost for half a measure and skipped a few notes. But because I had learned the piece well, I knew what came next, my hand found its place within a couple of beats, and I kept playing as if nothing had happened.

A year later, while performing the Ravel Concerto in G with the Denver Symphony, I had a similar experience. In the first movement, I mistakenly played a half measure of a passage in the wrong key, a key in which it appears later in the movement. Instantly recognizing my mistake, I jumped back to the proper key without missing a beat. Later in the same movement, I played a couple of wrong notes because I suddenly forgot the right ones, and then went on as usual. When the performance was over, the conductor congratulated me on how well I played. I said, "What about those things that went wrong?" "Oh, those little things in the first movement?" he replied. "Those things happen to everybody."

These two experiences gave me confidence and helped me relax about playing from memory. We can't turn ourselves into computers that never break down and never forget the program, and we don't have to. We can allow for human error, and through thorough study of the music, we can create a safety net to catch us if we falter in performance.

We can also demystify the scary animal we call memorization and make friends with it by learning how it works—what its parts are, what kind of food it eats, and what kind of exercise it needs to stay in shape.

Types of Memory

In teaching adult beginners, I have learned how much we take for granted when making music is second nature to us. At a first or second lesson, the adult student, trying to coordinate two hands and one foot while reading the music, finding his way around the keyboard, and keeping time, typically looks aghast and exclaims, "There are so many things to think about!"

When we try to memorize music, we often have a similar experience. We remember one hand more than the other, or we remember the sound of the music better than which keys or strings we have to use to produce the sound. The piece falls apart because we haven't completely put it together. We realize how many different elements we have to master. We have to integrate several types of memory to learn one piece.

We are all familiar with kinesthetic memory, also known as muscle memory. In the middle of playing or singing a piece, our mind wanders, and although we are unaware of what's happening in the music, our fingers keep moving and spinning out the right notes at the right time. Our body knows what to do because it has done it so many times before.

Relying solely on kinesthetic memory is dangerous, because if the body slips up, you don't know where you are in the score, and you have to do what the famous pianist did in San Francisco—start all over from the beginning. Having had enough experience with this problem by the time I was seventeen, I tried memorizing Franck's Symphonic Variations through intellectual analysis of the score. I labeled intervals and chords with symbols, studied the patterns they made, and committed streams of complex chromatic melodies and harmonies to memory.

When I went to my lesson with Menahem Pressler, he noticed that each time I played a certain passage I used a different fingering. I could play the piece from memory, but my *hands* hadn't completely memorized it. He circled the passage in my score, wrote "finger memory" on the page, and told me that I must train my hands to know the music. In subsequent lessons, he tested me on my kinesthetic memory by playing part of this piece on the second piano, stopping in the middle of a phrase, and asking me to continue playing from where he left off.

From then on, I began using mental rehearsal—I went through pieces in my head, imagining playing each key with the correct finger, to make sure I knew every note and every fingering from memory. If I got stuck at any point in this mental process, I picked up the score, marked the place I didn't know in colored pencil, and studied it. I remember lying on the bed in my dormitory room at Indiana University the day before a competition on Ravel's G major concerto and going through the entire piece in my head three times. Then I went through the right hand alone three times, followed by the left hand alone three times.

I have never since gone to that extreme in mentally rehearsing a piece, and looking back, it may have been a little compulsive. But I was curious: I wanted to know if I could do it, if I could discipline my mind to that extent. I needed to see how far I could stretch myself, and it gave me confidence for the competition.

None of this great effort to memorize music means anything if you can't hear it in your mind's ear while you mentally

219

go through the motions. A strong auditory memory not only helps you remember where to place your fingers but also creates a more musical performance. Can you imagine committing so much information to memory without knowing how it sounds?

Musicians with highly trained ears, or those who have perfect pitch, have a distinct advantage in performing from memory: If their kinesthetic or intellectual memory suddenly fails them, they can find the notes by listening to the sound in their head. Taking the time to use the listening techniques outlined in Chapter 10, so that you can hear every sound you are playing or singing with maximum sensitivity, will help you absorb music on a deep level and reinforce it in your memory.

Some musicians also have a photographic memory and can picture the printed page in their mind with every note precisely in its place. If you are gifted with this special ability, it can come in handy in performance.

Familiarity, Meaning, and Memory

We tend to remember things that are familiar to us. We know the way to the grocery store because we've taken it before, and we recall some of our parents' words of advice because we have heard them so many times. Similarly, we may find that simply practicing a piece instills most of it in our memory.

We also remember things that have special meaning for us. I don't think I will ever forget some of my husband's thoughtful words on our first date, or the heartbroken look our cat gave us when we visited him in the animal hospital and then had to say good-bye. Many things we remember we would rather forget: the sound of cruel words spoken to us, the sight of a mother slapping her child on the street, or the pain of hurting our best friend's feelings when we are impatient or insensitive. All of these experiences, positive and negative alike, make an indelible impression on the heart.

Musical memory is often the same: The more a piece affects our heart, the more easily we remember it. Whatever degree of natural ability we have, learning music by heart comes from opening our heart to each sound we hear and each movement we make. In the Art of Practicing, we practice deep receptiveness to music and movement. We take time to cultivate emotional vulnerability, mental clarity, physical ease, and vivid listening. All of these elements become integrated and work together.

Becoming a Vehicle for the Music

When you open to music in this way, it enters your system. It lives within you and can naturally flow out in performance. You thus become a vehicle for the composer's work, capable of transmitting it to others. Becoming a vehicle doesn't mean that you ignore your own feelings or restrict your self-expression. It means you expand your feeling capacity by becoming receptive to the wealth of details in a composition.

The common argument over the virtue of "being true to the composer" versus giving the music "your personal interpretation" (or "putting your personal stamp on it") contains a fundamental misconception about music-making. If you love a particular Beethoven sonata and you take the time to learn it thoroughly, no conflict exists between you and Beethoven at that point. You don't have to worry about whether or not your personal qualities will come through in your performance. On the contrary, your heart, your love for the composer and his work, shines through every note he wrote. You meet his mind and are not separate from him. In performance, you and Beethoven come alive for your audience simultaneously.

Such performing is confident. Because the music lives within you, you can present it to others with a sense of natural command. Whether you are an amateur or a professional, you can achieve this mastery of a piece of music. You can play or sing by heart.

QUESTIONS AND ANSWERS

Question: *Some musicians can memorize a piece directly from the score before they ever play it. Is that what you mean by memorizing music intellectually? Do you just look at the score and analyze it, like a music-theory assignment?*

Answer: People who learn music without having to play it are not simply memorizing the notes; they can hear the notes in their mind's ear. So instead of just analyzing the score, they are hearing the music and feeling it inside them.

Intellectual learning need not be done in a dry, A-B-C-D kind of way, but in conjunction with an internal experience of the music. You don't just memorize notes; you memorize the feeling of playing them, the phrasing, the emotional content—everything at once. And in addition to remembering the music, you need to imagine the hand placements and movements so that your body learns the piece to some extent.

Practicing and memorizing are about amalgamating information with spontaneity. The Art of Practicing cultivates spontaneity, and studying the different elements in a piece allows you to integrate the storing of facts with the experience of spontaneous flow. When you perform, it all works together. If you lose the sense of flow and have a memory lapse, your factual mind, or left brain, takes over and supplies the information you need to get back on course.

Question: *I once memorized a piece in sections so my brain could handle a little at a time. I knew each section, but I didn't work much on the connections between one section and the next. Then I panicked in the concert and lost my place. Is it possible to grasp a whole piece and memorize it without breaking it up into sections?*

Answer: Feeding your brain bite-size pieces is a natural way of learning music. Unless you have a memory like Mozart's, you can absorb only so much at a time. But you need to have the whole design of the piece rooted in your system so that those bites add up to a satisfying meal.

One of my childhood piano teachers taught me to memorize the beginning of each section of a piece so that I would know places to jump to if my mind blanked in performance. I didn't like this method; studying a series of disconnected beginnings and committing them to memory took the joy out of learning for me. But for some people this technique may work well. In any case, if you study the music thoroughly, you become aware of which notes begin each section.

In addition to practicing a section at a time, make a relationship with the whole composition by studying its form. Much of your feeling for the broad structure will come naturally from working with the principles of organizing music into phrases and textures and discovering how one phrase leads to another. Get used to playing through the work from beginning to end so that you develop a feeling for how it unfolds in time.

Question: *Once I know a piece by heart I get lost if I try to perform it from the score. What can I do about that?*

Answer: I had a similar experience preparing for a live radio broadcast. A couple of days before the performance, I panicked about having a memory lapse on the air with thousands of people listening, and since I would be playing in the radio studio and the audience couldn't see me, I decided to use the score. I felt relieved once I had made this decision, until I tried playing from the score in my living room and my hands suddenly became uncoordinated in several passages. I realized I needed to become accustomed to the feeling of looking at the printed page while playing.

Performing from memory usually brings a sense of freedom because you're not busy looking at the little black dots. You can let go more easily. But if you plan to look at the score during performance in order to feel more secure, practice that way. Then you'll be more comfortable onstage.

Question: *I'm an amateur musician, and I've never memorized the pieces I study. Do I need to learn how?*
Answer: Only if you want to. Even professional musicians didn't perform from memory until Franz Liszt introduced the practice in the nineteenth century. When you study a piece for a long time, memorization usually comes fairly naturally. But many amateurs prefer to move on to new repertoire before they've absorbed a piece to that extent. And some professionals prefer the security of having the score in front of them even if they know it by heart. If you get curious about what it would be like to play a piece from memory, try it. You'll get to know the music better and you may enjoy the freedom of not having to focus on the printed page. It's up to you. "Amateur" means one who loves something. Do what you love.

Question: *I'm trained in Renaissance music, in which if you play the notes that are written, you're not playing the music. It's like playing jazz. Is that different from becoming a vehicle for the music?*
Answer: I don't play Renaissance music, but even if you're improvising, you still must follow a form; you still have to go by

a particular set of rules to create an organic whole. In that sense, you make yourself into a vehicle for the style of that period.

Question: *How is being a vehicle different from being an interpreter?*

Answer: People often think the performer's role is to think up imaginative ideas about a piece that nobody else would think of and that would make his performance valid as a unique phenomenon. He presents his version, or his interpretation, of the music to the audience, and that version is often a distortion of the original.

Being a vehicle, on the other hand, means you surrender distorted views and take in the piece as it is, letting it permeate your system, so that the listeners receive the genuine article, a fine piece of music revealed by a fine performer. When you make yourself receptive to the written notes, however, you also respond to them with your own understanding and body energy. So you become the agent who breathes life into the music, and you create a unique interpretation in that sense.

When a performer studies a piece in depth, he sometimes becomes a better vehicle for it than the composer himself. Stravinsky's works, for instance, often sound better in the hands of another conductor than in his own recorded performances of them. It's as though the composer looked in the mirror and failed to perceive some of his own appeal. So you could consider yourself a lover of the composer, with the intention of appreciating and understanding his work as much as you can so that it shines in your presence.

CHAPTER 14

Generosity

On the day of my New York debut in 1984 I had a pain in my chest near my heart that persisted for a few hours. I called my wisest friend and told her I felt I was going to die. "You probably are," she said. "You won't be the same person when this concert is over." More than any other concert I had played, the debut was a moment of truth for me. Though I felt ready to present myself to the world as a pianist, I couldn't know if I would feel confident when I actually set foot onstage.

I called a second wise friend, who said, "Put on your dress and go down there." Make it real, he meant. Being a performer himself, he knew about these things. I put on the red gown and matching shoes and felt better. The car I had ordered the day before pulled up in front of my apartment building at six-fifteen and took me to Carnegie Recital Hall. I went in, greeted my piano tuner, did my hair, and warmed up on the Steinway grand I had selected a few days earlier. The concrete, ordered reality of the clothes, car, hall, piano, and piano tuner calmed me down. At the precise hour, the house lights dimmed, and with the first step I took into the light onstage, my nervous excitement broke into exhilaration. I was at home. I knew I belonged there. I knew it without a doubt for the first time.

The concert went well and received a fine review. But my wisest friend was right: I was not the same person after that. Having discovered that I possessed the confidence I had hoped for, I began thinking about other aspects of my life. My fulfillment as a performer made the unfulfilling parts of my life painfully obvious in contrast.

I felt at home onstage but not in the everyday world. What I loved about performing was the chance to give. It took me into the core of my generosity and brought a feeling of oneness with the audience and the composer. I wanted more of that experience of giving and sharing outside of performing. Several months after the debut, I started teaching the Art of Practicing, began focusing intensely on my personal relationships, and gave up performing. It was the biggest shock of my life.

We have one lifetime in which to express ourselves and to connect to others. A performance is in that sense a microcosm of life: We have one chance, and we want to give it everything we have. When we give freely, we experience our passion and vitality, which is a gift to us in return. We get frightened at the moment of performance not only because we want to do well but because we feel so alive. We fear life itself, the feeling of our heart beating, of letting music and vital energy flow through us beyond our control. We are walking containers of life, and when we walk onto a stage to perform, we feel that intensely.

Every courageous act we commit in life transforms us in some way. When we take our place onstage shaking with fear and dare to make music, we re-create not only a musical composition but also ourselves. We give in to the power of life, which is bigger than we are, and become bigger through that surrender. We discover we can allow the rushing river of music, fear, and vitality to run through us. We can abandon ourselves to it and survive in one piece.

Transforming Fear into Fearlessness

Some performers try to protect themselves from fear by pretending they're alone in the hall, with no audience present. They feel threatened by the audience, so they ignore the rows of people who have come to enjoy fine music and have welcomed them with applause. Other performers try to avoid fear by directing their music-making toward one particular audience member and shutting out the rest.

Fear is energy. If you allow it to flow through you, you transform it into fearlessness. Bravery doesn't mean that you don't feel afraid. If it did, you'd have nothing to be brave about. It's when you feel frightened of a situation but step into it anyway that you demonstrate courage. Each time you confront fear head on and let the adrenaline flood your body, you liberate the energy of fear and make it available for creative action. The man proposing marriage, the performer facing an audience, the new person in a group speaking up for the first time, all are courageous human beings. At the moment they take the next step by expressing their heart and mind, they transform fear into fearlessness. In doing so, they transform themselves.

Sometimes we're afraid of failure. We have something at stake and we want to come out ahead. We can also be afraid of success. We are used to thinking of ourselves in a particular way, and if we take a leap into a new situation, it may change our lives in a way that threatens our familiar definition of ourselves. In any case, we're afraid of the unknown in ourselves, of the self deep inside that is about to rise to the surface and become known—visible, audible, palpable. If we don't continually give birth to ourselves through creative acts, we perpetuate a fearful existence. We can keep growing only if we face our fear and dare to step forward through it.

My student Alan, who is in his fifties, came to a lesson two months into his chemotherapy treatments for cancer and announced that he was retiring from teaching piano so that he could devote his time to practicing and performing. He proceeded to play a Chopin ballade with a freedom and élan beyond anything I had ever heard from him. His usual shoulder tension was gone, the music seemed to rush with an electric charge through his arms, and he projected a sense of command and confidence. When he finished playing and heard my compliments, he said, "I feel so vulnerable and terrified. I just made this decision that I would rather perform than teach, and I've never thought of myself as a real performer. Now I'm being one, and it terrifies me." "That explains the fantastic freedom in your playing," I said. "You're feeling your fear and playing anyway. You're transforming fear into fearlessness."

The Bravery to Be Who We Are

Performing is an action: We are *doing* something special, and the audience is watching every move we make. We develop an inner spectator in our mind, imagining a performance before it takes place. As we picture ourselves in front of the audience, we think, "I don't know if I can do it." Doing it frightens us.

Courageous doing arises from courageous being. In addition to giving an audience music, we give them ourselves. We give who we are at that moment, and every performance is unique because we grow in between performances; we are not exactly the same person we were last time. The cells and breath in our body are new, fresh, and unpredictable. We are also affected by the particular audience and atmosphere of the moment. We can't control them; we can't even tell where we leave off and they begin. All the energy mixes together.

A musician friend of mine once said about performing, "You never know what your body is going to do." We have to abandon ourselves to what is happening in the moment. We must let the energy in our body be as it is and let our actions arise spontaneously from that energy.

When I give a seminar on the Art of Practicing, it feels like a performance. I have presented the same material many times, but it resonates differently in my mind each time and I never know exactly what words will come out of my mouth or in what tone or rhythm I will speak them. I am always surprised by the quality of the energy in my body and the sound of my voice. Sometimes I feel I have nothing special to offer that day, but I give an exceptionally good talk. Sometimes I sense a quiet, focused quality in my mind beforehand, and an unexpectedly colorful presentation comes out. We don't know where performance energy comes from. But if we open up, it comes through us. Life comes through.

Preparing to Transmit the Energy

To transmit energy to others, the energy within you must be fluid and free to flow out. The preparatory steps before practicing—stretching, settling in, and tuning into your heart—are all helpful before performing. Find a place offstage where you can be alone and gather your forces. You don't need to stretch on the floor in your fancy clothes, but allow yourself the luxury of releasing pent-up tensions by doing a few good stretches, as many as you like.

To settle in, you may want to take more time than you usually do before practicing. I like to sit and focus on my breathing for twenty minutes before addressing a group, but even two minutes will help. Experiment and see what works well for you.

Your heart is likely to be open when you're about to play or sing for others; you feel vulnerable. The tuning-in exercise you've done before practicing, of reflecting on the impermanence of life, may not be necessary now because you are keenly aware that you have only one chance in this performance—the rehearsals are over and you're in the spotlight. What's needed is to rouse confidence in your ability to give.

Rousing confidence starts with appreciating yourself as you are, extending warmth to yourself so that you can extend it naturally to the music and to others. Whatever is going on in your life on that day—whether you are happy or sad, whether you feel good or bad about events in your life—you need to make contact with your own goodness, your heart, in order to make contact with the hearts of your listeners. This process can take place in a few minutes, or it can require months or years of preparation, depending on your personal strength and experience and on how much importance you attach to a particular performance.

Self-doubt

Sometimes we feel vibrant and ready to give our hearts to others in performance. At other times, discouraging people in our life or the fear of a hostile critic in the audience makes us shrink and lose heart. Occasionally, a particular performance means so much to us that it puts us through the wringer in a way that has never happened before. The novice performer presenting himself to an audience for the first time, the young artist entering a competition, and the seasoned performer about to appear as soloist with a major orchestra, all may become especially anxious during the days, weeks, or months prior to their big moment.

In the middle of writing this final chapter I became panic-stricken. The book would soon be completed and sent out into the world. My writing suddenly felt like a performance, and performance anxiety hit me full force. I thought to myself, "Do I really know what to say about performing? Do I have anything to offer my readers?" I began to live the material I was writing about. I sat in the corner of the room and imagined my book in print, with the title and my name on the cover, occupying a place on neatly organized shelves in bookstores and in the hands of many different people. "Do I really have what it takes to reach these people?" I thought. "Who am I anyway? I've always thought of myself as a performer, a person who addresses large groups of people and feels potent with material, with life energy. Why do I suddenly feel as though I have nothing to say?" For two weeks, I felt I was swimming in a sea of doubt and confusion with nothing to hold on to.

Finally, I realized I had to bring these feelings into the writing of this chapter. I am scared of change, of my unknown future as an author and teacher in the public eye. As I approach the moment of being in the spotlight, all my insecurities, including some I didn't know I had, seem to stand out in a spotlight of their own. I feel more ordinary than ever.

My frightened mind rambled on: "Do I have enough understanding of the subject? Can I say what I have to say in a way that will help people and inspire them? Do other authors feel this way, or am I just feeling afraid because I don't belong out there? Can I tell my readers I'm panicking and expect *that* to touch their hearts and minds? Can I tell them I feel like a frightened child at times and that I don't know how I'll get it together to address them like an adult?"

How can we present ourselves to others when we feel exposed, when the most private things about us are written all over our face or come through in every note or every word we produce?

A performance is an intimate act. The specific content of our thoughts may not be perceived by the audience, but the blood and adrenaline running through our body communicate to them. A published book, with an elegant cover and neat type, can contain the author's vital energy, and in spite of a tuxedo or long gown, a performer can feel emotionally naked. The ordered formality of presenting ourselves to the public accentuates the rawness we feel inside, the tenderness of our nerves.

Intimacy with Ourselves: Facing the Demons

The intimacy of making music for others necessitates an intimacy with ourselves, a willingness to open up and experience ourselves in depth. As we approach the moment of performance, we often find ourselves grappling with negative forces within us that go beyond simple self-doubt.

To one degree or another, we each have our private inner demons that intimidate us at crucial moments. Some performers can relax and let go onstage in front of the public but panic at an audition. The knowledge that they are being judged brings up deep-seated beliefs that they are inadequate and deserve to fail. Performing and auditioning bring our demons out of hiding and force us to confront them. We have a golden opportunity to exorcise these demons by seeing them clearly, becoming familiar with them, and working our way through the jungle they inhabit.

In the movie *Postcards from the Edge,* Meryl Streep portrays a Hollywood actress/singer whose competitive mother, also an actress/singer, has intimidated her to the point where she is unable to perform with confidence. After years of not believing in herself and seeking solace in drugs, she unleashes her anger in a conversation with her mother, who is forced to listen and to admit her own weakness. The daughter makes peace with her mother and feels whole and strong for the first time. The movie closes with a scene of her onstage before a crowd, singing exuberantly, all stops pulled out, and her proud mother watching. The frightened, hurt, confused little girl has turned herself into a gutsy, fully alive woman, spreading her joy freely and gloriously.

In real life, we may not have the opportunity to vent our rage at an external tormentor, or it may not be appropriate to do so. But we must recognize the torment within us and let ourselves feel not only our fear but also the pain and anger that naturally arise when healthy self-expression is obstructed. Psychotherapist Diane Nichols, director of the Performing Arts Psychotherapy Center in New York, describes a variety of destructive influences on young performers. Not only competitive parents but overly critical parents and teachers, or parents who ignore their child's talent, can undermine confidence. Problems also arise when parents show more interest in their child's talent than in the child as a person. All of these situations create conflict and anger within the child that may surface in adulthood and may require psychotherapy to resolve. Left unresolved, such feelings may result in excessive or debilitating performance anxiety.[1]

Anger can be a particularly difficult emotion to deal with. No matter how understandable our anger may be at times, we are often discouraged from expressing it or even feeling it because of its destructive power. But anger has its proper place and time. Our joyous music-making energy is sacred, and so is the wrath that rises in its defense. A musician friend of mine once said, "If you're a performer, your vulnerability is your product." We walk onstage offering our hearts to whoever is present. Anger is a natural response to any force that works against the triumph of that vulnerability.

In my twenties, I once had to give a solo recital on the same day that a man I loved told me he didn't want to be with me. I sat backstage forty minutes before the concert crying and wondering how I would get myself together to perform. Finally, I became angry that my concert might be ruined on account of some unappreciative guy. I told myself, "You love him because you have a good heart. Go out there and show them how good it is." My sorrow turned to joy, and I played with abandon.

When we give anger the room to explode like a volcano inside our body, we liberate our spirit for making music. As artists, we need access to all of our emotional energies. Even if we are playing a simple, lyrical tune, having a "tiger in our tank," a fierceness that is ready to stand up for our heart if anyone rejects or violates it, allows us to speak our heart with strength, clarity, and focus. The softest, most tender message can penetrate the listener's heart like an arrow.

Appreciating Your Own Goodness

Fear of performing includes an excitement about giving something to our audience. My student Ned told me at his lesson one day that he always gets nervous on the day of a lesson. "I want you to be proud of me," he said. "I guess it's just ego." "No, it isn't," I told him. "What do you really think it is?" He thought a moment and answered, "We have a relationship. When you teach me something, you give me a gift. I take it home and make it my own, and then I want to give it back to you. Your thing becomes my thing, and when I play for you, it's our thing." His words touched me. In expressing his devotion as my student, he fueled my devotion as his teacher. I wanted to give to him even more than before. He thus demonstrated the self-perpetuating nature of generosity he had described.

In addition to giving something to our listeners, we want them to see and hear who we are, and to receive their appreciation in return. They give us the opportunity to express ourselves, and we get nervous partly because we want to show them the best of who we are. This desire is not merely egocentric; it comes from self-respect and from appreciating the opportunity to connect to others, to be part of human society.

When you are about to perform, whether for your teacher or for thousands of people, take a moment to appreciate your desire to make music for others. Such desire is healthy and good. Appreciating your own goodness is a way of extending friendship to yourself. It will generate the warmth you need for communicating with your audience.

Confidence and the Circulation of Energy

Facing our fears, doubts, and demons brings out our strength, and appreciating our goodness cultivates tenderness. Together this strength and tenderness become confidence: We have conviction in our heart's power.

In 1992, I was invited to participate in a training program in Vermont to become a teacher of Shambhala Training, a secular approach to meditation practice. Two months before the program, each participant was assigned two challenging topics and asked to prepare short talks on them. During those two months I spent hours every day studying my assigned topics and preparing my talks. At the program, each participant gave one talk to a small group the first afternoon. The same evening, three of us were selected to each present our second talk to the entire group of trainees and staff in the formal meditation hall. After announcing my name, the program director gave me two minutes to collect myself in the next room before coming in to address the group.

I had worked hard, and I was nervous and excited about giving this special presentation. I thought of my meditation teacher and everything he had given me, and I was filled with longing to do well, to honor his faith in me, and to carry on his tradition by giving a piece of it to others. Suddenly I felt a rush of confident energy rise up inside me and carry me into the hall, as if I had been lifted onto a magic carpet. I sensed that because my longing was so strong, this unexpected energy had become available to me. It continued to flow throughout my presentation.

Being at the center of attention doesn't mean you have to be self-centered. On the contrary, your devotion to the music and the audience will magnetize people more than an arrogant attitude. Everyone is naturally more attracted to an openhearted person than to an egotist. From your first step into the spotlight, let your heart take center stage. As the audience greets you with applause, open your heart to the energy around you. Take time to keep your balance amidst your excitement by taking notice of simple things, such as how your feet feel as you walk, or how the light hits the stage. Enjoy bowing, take your time sitting down, and notice how it feels to sit in your seat. If you're performing with other musicians, be aware of them and of their need to settle themselves, too. Notice the atmosphere in the hall. Notice your nervous energy. Take a moment to let yourself breathe.

Composing yourself this way sets the tone for the audience. They think, "This person's taking time to settle down and breathe. I can, too." They need transition time after their day and after talking among themselves. Before your entrance, they may have been discussing new purchases or family problems. If you dive into your program when their minds are still on the events of their day, they don't have a chance to unwind. But if you enter and situate yourself with warmth and calm dignity, you can help them relax. Your presence transforms the atmosphere into one in which people can forget about the workaday world, make contact with their hearts, and open to music. This is the beginning of your gift to them.

After you have settled yourself, notice the atmosphere enveloping you. You are about to make music in this expectant space, and if you are aware of the space the music will enter, you will sense how and when to begin. When the moment comes, focus on the music you're about to play or sing, make your first move, and let the music come. The stronger your heart intention is, the easier it will be to let the music flow and to accommodate what is happening around you. Distracting sounds from the audience and your own self-conscious thoughts become manageable when you open up and focus on expressing yourself.

Sometimes we have self-critical thoughts while performing: "I botched that section! I'm terrible!" Or we may puff ourselves up with praise: "I certainly played that section well! Aren't I terrific!" The chatter of critical and arrogant thoughts tends to dissolve in the heat of the desire to communicate. Nevertheless, *some* thoughts are likely to float through our minds during performance. Perhaps we just find ourselves making odd observations like, "My sleeves feel funny on my arms," or, "What a strange light that is on the curtain over there."

We need to view our thoughts with a sense of humor. We're human, and our minds tend to wander and to pass judgment on our behavior. We can communicate with an audience in spite of our random thoughts. Magic can happen amid the ordinary reality of how our clothes feel against our skin and how our minds chatter. If we take our thoughts too seriously, we get caught up in them and lose touch with our heart and with the main event that is taking place. When that connection is lost, we may even lose our place in the music. But if we take a light, friendly attitude toward our thoughts and just let them come and go as they habitually do, we can maintain a sense of command and confidence.

Our job as performers is to accommodate everything that arises in our awareness—our extraneous thoughts, coughs from the audience, the lights, our fear, and our excitement, as well as the music. If we can do that, if we can give all the energy of the moment a perpetual green light to run through us as it will, an electric current passes between us and our listeners. We receive and transmit the vitality in that space at that moment.

In spite of the spontaneity of this experience, being confident and freely transmitting energy to others doesn't always feel good. We may find ourselves playing or singing a piece quite differently from the way we have before, which may confuse us and lead us to judge our performance negatively. I remember making a videotape of Schubert's G-flat impromptu. Nine bars into the first take, I stopped playing because it felt draggy and dull. I then did five complete takes, which sounded much better to me. When I heard the tape, I was stunned. The nine bars I had started with were wonderful, and all five of the complete takes were disappointing and unusable. I wished I had let myself finish playing the piece the first time.

My student Greg was similarly unaware of how well he played Chopin's B-flat minor nocturne at his lesson one day. His performance of the piece usually had rough edges, but this time I was shocked by the smoothness and beauty of the sound. I felt as though I were bathing in cognac. When he finished playing, I asked him, "So how much do you want me to pay you for listening to that?" He burst into tears. He said he didn't know he was performing well—that he was in a state of turmoil while playing because he felt raw and exposed. "When I've exposed myself that way before," he explained, "people have gone away. But you're paying me a supreme compliment." It gave him new confidence to discover that his real, vulnerable self could make such beautiful music.

Even the most seasoned artists can experience inner turmoil while performing. I once went backstage to tell a famous pianist I know how wonderfully he had just played Beethoven's Fourth Piano Concerto. "Really?" he said. "I went through a lot out there. I couldn't tell."

Celebration

The grandness of presentation that challenges and frightens us in performance also honors our vulnerability. We dress up in fine clothes to give a concert because we are celebrating the power that emanates from an exposed human heart.

Sometimes we see a performer's vulnerability clearly when she walks onstage. I remember a TV movie in which a popular singer was making a comeback after not performing in public for several years. She didn't know if she could rise to the occasion, and when she entered in her gown and faced the audience, her hands shook and a look of fear spread across her face. The first notes came out a little shaky, but that shakiness soon gave way to a warm, expansive performance. I was thrilled as much by her daring as by the wonderful music she made.

I had a similar experience hearing a young boy from the Harlem Boys Choir sing a solo one night in New York's Central Park. I didn't know the choir would be performing; like the half million other people who had gathered in the park on that warm, summer evening, I had come to hear a recital by Luciano Pavarotti. But halfway through the concert, Mr. Pavarotti took a break, and the boys walked onstage. When the solo came, we could see the performer's sweet, innocent face clearly on the giant video screen in front of the crowd. He sang with a soft, pure sound and seemed to capture everyone's attention even more than the famous tenor had. This child's bravery in singing simply and quietly to the throngs of people who had come not to hear him but to hear a superstar touched me deeply. When he finished singing, the half million people burst into heartfelt applause and cheering.

Ensemble Performing

Ensemble performing celebrates the human heart in a special way. When our subtle musical impulses and rhythms meld with those of another performer, we experience an intimacy akin to lovemaking. When we perform in a large ensemble, we experience a heightening of our devotion to music through expressing that devotion simultaneously with many other musicians.

One of my students once performed as a flutist in a university orchestra. The conductor was a clarinetist who was an excellent musician but had little conducting training or experience; he had simply been given the job, at the last moment, of leading the orchestra that season. The first rehearsals went badly. The orchestra members had no respect for this man and refused to cooperate. Finally, one day he put down his baton and said, "Listen. *I* know I'm not a conductor and *you* know I'm not a conductor. But let's put our heads together and see what we can do." Moved by his honesty, the group instantly became inspired to do their best. They all contributed ideas about how to play the music, and they worked together enthusiastically for several weeks. On concert night, they uncorked a hair-raising performance. Such magic occurs when we let boundaries between us dissolve and give ourselves over to the passion of making music.

CONCLUSION

Our need to give is as strong as our need to receive. We are given life and music, and the richer we feel with these gifts, the more we want to share them with others. Performing, a form of sharing, multiplies our gifts by transforming us and enriching our audience at the same time. This is our work and our celebration.

QUESTIONS AND ANSWERS

Question: *If you love the music and the audience and you want to communicate, why should you be afraid?*
Answer: Precisely because you care so much, and you can't control what will happen. In practice or rehearsal, you can stop and redo a passage if it doesn't go well, but in performance, you can't. You have one chance to bring your work to fruition, and it matters what happens this particular time.
Q: *I read that when Jacqueline du Pré was asked how she felt before she walked onstage, she said, "I can't wait to get out there." Do you feel like that?*
A: Yes.
Q: *Are you also scared?*
A: Yes. It's natural to be both excited and scared about taking a risk. But I feel at home in a performing situation. It's liberating to know that I have the freedom to let go of controls and express myself.

Question: *Do you think that liberated feeling comes with a lot of exposure, or also after exploring your feelings about your relationship to an audience—what the audience means to you and what performing means to you?*

Answer: Exposure helps, but it's the quality of your experience, not just how many times you've performed, that is most important. If you have a deep understanding of performing and you make a commitment to it, you will be more ready to relate to the audience. You need generosity to the music, to yourself, and to the audience.

Question: *I'm going to be uncomfortable playing in your workshop because I haven't played in public for two years. For one year I didn't play at all, and playing has been a constant struggle for me. I'm afraid I might even stop in the middle, or that I'll become hysterical. I also haven't had as much time to practice as I wanted to lately, so I don't feel prepared. How can I get myself to focus?*

Answer: Usually we go in and out of focus even if we're well prepared. Ideally, we have faith in our preparation and can relax somewhat about performing. If you don't feel prepared, you have to accept that; you don't have an ideal situation. Appreciate the fact that you've come here to learn something and to develop yourself. And appreciate your willingness to present yourself as you are. It's a generous thing to do. Extending warmth to yourself can help you relax and focus.

In admitting how you feel, you're already giving something to others. When one person admits she has difficulties, it helps other people. They realize they're not the only ones who are afraid, and they feel less alone.

Question: *Sometimes I get tense trying to play a strange piano in a concert or audition, especially if I don't have a chance to try out the instrument ahead of time. How should I deal with that situation?*

Answer: It takes me forty-five minutes to adjust to a strange piano. If you can't arrange that much time before a performance, at least run your hand over the keys and get a sense of how stiff or loose the action is. In an audition situation, you may be allowed to play a chord to get an idea of the basic sound so you aren't totally thrown by what comes out when you start to play.

John Crown, with whom I studied at the University of Southern California, advised me never to attempt to over-adjust to any piano. If it has a small sound, forcing it will just make you tight. If it sounds too loud, trying hard to play soft will also make you tight. The audience will feel your tension. You're better off giving up your expectations and relaxing with the instrument you have. Then your body will be free, and you'll communicate more.

For an important concert, it pays to rent an instrument you feel comfortable with. When I went to rehearse in the hall for my New York debut, I found a different piano onstage from the one that had been there the year before. The action was too stiff for me. I tried to get used to it, but after practicing on this instrument for two hours I went across the street to Steinway Hall and selected a special piano for my big night.

Question: *In interviews, Horowitz comes across as an egomaniac. He says things like, "I was so great—they really loved me," and, "I was the greatest thing you ever heard." But don't you have to feel that way if you're going to get up and play? Everybody is out to get you; they're out to rip you apart. If you don't think you're the greatest, how can you do it?*

Answer: Horowitz may have said these things *after* a performance, but it is well known that he experienced intense fear before going onstage. You need humility to perform, which means accepting yourself as you are. If your attitude is that they're out to get you and that you have to put up defenses, you can't open up and be generous. But if you think, "Maybe one person wants me to fall on my face but the rest of them just want their hearts touched," you have a chance of doing something good.

Basically, people want you to do well. When you go to a concert, are you hoping that the performer is going to do a bad job so that you've wasted your money? Do you spend your money to see people fail? I don't think so. If it's Tuesday night, and you're exhausted, and you go to the Philharmonic, you don't want it to be a disaster. You want to have a good time. People go to concerts because they want to be uplifted and re-vived, to feel like human beings. And that happens only if the performer is willing to share his or her humanity with other people, which means being vulnerable.

If you're making music for others, you don't have to think that you have your act together a hundred percent; you just have to be generous. You can always tell when a performer has that sense of humanity. His presence fills the hall. People don't just want to hear the music played or sung a certain way; they want to witness someone being truly human. Then they can feel wonderful about being human themselves.

We also want to feel our own human response to a per-former, to let his vulnerability touch our heart. In our techno-logical age, we often lose sight of this reason for leaving our home and going to a concert. "It's easier to put on a CD," we may think. Or, "I can see it better on TV." But going to a con-cert hall and sharing a fine performance with other people can energize and inspire us in a way that a recording or broadcast cannot. I have seen the most competitive music students and professionals, who analyze other people's performances and try to bolster their own egos by finding fault, lose interest in their critical agendas when they attend a moving perfor-mance.

Question: *Sometimes I hear discouraging voices in my head before an important performance. I hear my parents and one of my teachers saying, "You shouldn't try to play such a big concert. You're not good enough, and you never will be." Then anger takes hold of me, and I can never really resolve it. I feel that if it weren't for these people, I'd be a more confident performer. How can I get over my anger?*

Answer: You're describing what happens when we get caught up in blaming others for our problems. Other people do affect our lives, but placing blame complicates the experience of being angry. In addition to feeling the raw emotion of anger, we get caught in a desire to prove that someone is wrong and to get back at them in some way.

I've found that when I'm angry, the key to getting over it is to focus less on the object of the anger and more on the pure energy of the emotion, to recognize that the rage is mine and that I have a right to it. If I let myself feel the explosive energy completely, it often dissolves quickly. If it doesn't, I try to stay with it a little longer or to find an appropriate way to express it.

Anger contains a lot of power. It can be difficult to handle, and I consider myself a beginner at working with it skillfully. It's like riding a wild horse: You can do damage if you don't have command of it. Or you can simply wear yourself out struggling with it and end up going around in circles instead of moving forward.

You have a right to be angry, but try switching your focus away from the people you hold responsible. It's *your* emotion. You need to focus on your wild energy, to become familiar with it and take full possession of it so that you can harness it. This is a demanding job, so be patient with yourself. You will probably fall off the horse many times; just get back on and try again. Little by little, you can learn to keep your seat when the horse runs amok and to channel its energy for good use.

Sometimes people try to discourage you because they lack confidence themselves. They don't understand how you can dare to do what you're doing because they can't picture themselves being so daring. They may even envy you for your talent or accomplishments. If you understand their feelings, you can develop compassion for them. This doesn't mean you have to stick around while they throw darts at you; you can walk away. But you can also realize that you are richer than they are because you have more confidence. This awareness can melt your anger and open your heart for performing.

Question: *I have a concert in two months, and I'm constantly worried if I'll be ready in time and if it will go well. How should I handle that?*
Answer: You'll probably worry until the concert is over, but that's all right. You can't know exactly how prepared you will be or how well you will play that night. Trust yourself in spite of your worry.
Q: *But I'm new in town, and I feel that with every step I take, I'm taking a risk and being judged.*
A: Some people may judge you. It's easy to judge others. It's harder to see the whole picture of their performance, to understand why they play a certain way and to relate intelligently and compassionately to their success or failure.

You may find you underestimated the amount of preparation time you needed, or you may realize after your performance that you could have played better if you had rested more and practiced less. In either situation, you gain valuable knowledge of yourself, and of the requirements of performing, that will help you in the future. Try to remember that your performance is important not only in itself but as part of your learning process. Every seasoned performer has lived through many mistakes and grown wiser from them.

You need to make friends. Find people who are going to be

there for you whether you make a mess out of your performance or not, people you can talk to about what you're going through, so that you're not always being judged and measured. They can help you cultivate your healthy intelligence, the voice within you that says, "I want to do well because I have something to give. I have a good heart, and I can learn from my mistakes."

Epilogue

In 1995, I attended a performance in Halifax by the Symphony Nova Scotia, conducted by composer Peter Lieberson. In the final work presented that evening, Brahms' First Symphony, the orchestra gave the most exciting musical performance I have ever heard. This monumental work came to life with such clarity, directness, passion, and abandon that Brahms' beating heart, in giant form, seemed to fill the hall. After the last note had sounded, the audience gave the musicians a long standing ovation. Many people spoke about the performance as enthusiastically as I did. With all the music we had heard in our lives, we didn't know that anything this sensational could occur.

Months later, I asked Mr. Lieberson to describe his experience preparing and conducting this performance. He spoke of the orchestra's complete commitment to the music in rehearsal and of how he had known and loved this symphony since he was eight years old. He had studied many different interpretations of it and had formed a definite idea of how it should be played. Nevertheless, he wasn't sure it would flow as he wanted it to in performance.

In rehearsal, the orchestra tended to lag behind his beat in the slow movement, and he was frustrated. Then he overheard one player saying to another, "If he'd only trust the orchestra more," and he realized that they would come along if he stopped trying so hard. Rehearsals went better after that, but at one point in the concert a whole section of players came in in a slower tempo than he wanted. After a moment of irritation, he relaxed, and the music suddenly flowed naturally. "It became blissful," he said.

Mr. Lieberson is not a professional conductor, and this orchestra was considerably smaller than the standard orchestra used to play a Brahms symphony. But he prefers a smaller group because he can hear the parts more clearly. The orchestra, in turn, was inspired to see a composer conduct the work of another composer with so much passion. Throughout the performance, he felt a strong rapport with the principal players, including the concertmaster, and had excellent visual communication with the orchestra. In addition to exchanging precise cues of nods and gestures with them, he noticed them radiating an enjoyment of the music. He particularly remembers one violinist smiling during a few bars' rest while he listened to lyrical phrases emanating from other instruments. The appreciation, trust, and communication between conductor and players added energy to the performance.

The audience also contributed energy. Our unusually enthusiastic response to the other works on the program infected the musicians with extra excitement.

Mr. Lieberson took many bows after this performance. Toward the end of our ovation, he picked up the score from his music stand, held it up, and pointed to it as if to say, "It's all in there. All we did was give you what he wrote." The score had a light blue cover, with black letters and an oval design on it. It looked thin and small, but the performers had revealed the genius it contained.

Notes

Chapter 2: Struggle and Freedom

1. Glenn Plaskin, "Learning from the Master," *M Magazine*, September 1985, p. 91.

Chapter 3: Stretching

1. Judith Scott, *Goodbye to Bad Backs: Stretching and Strengthening Exercises for Alignment and Freedom from Lower Back Pain,* 2d ed. (Pennington, N.J.: Dance Horizons/Princeton Book Company, 1993), p. 229
2. Ibid., p. 60.
3. Ibid., p. 56.
4. Ibid., p. 247.
5. Ibid., p. 47.

Chapter 6: Basic Mechanics

1. Barbara Conable and William Conable, *How to Learn the Alexander Technique: A Manual for Students* (Columbus, Ohio: Andover Road Press, 1992), p. 51.
2. Ibid., p. 85.
3. Wynn Kapit and Lawrence M. Elson, *The Anatomy Coloring Book* (New York: HarperCollins, 1977), plate 17.
4. Richard Norris, M.D., *A Musician's Survival Guide: A Guide to Preventing and Treating Injuries in Instrumentalists* (St. Louis, Mo.: International Conference of Symphony and Opera Musicians, 1993), pp. 59–61.

5. Ibid., p. 68.
6. Abby Whiteside, *The Indispensables of Piano Playing* (New York: Coleman-Ross Company, Inc., 1955), p. 74.
7. Ibid.
8. Jeffrey Solow, "Physically Efficient Cello Playing," in *Current Research in Arts and Medicine: A Compendium of the MedArt International 1992 World Congress on Arts and Medicine,* edited by Fadi J. Bejjani, M.D., Ph.D. (Pennington, N.J.: a cappella books, 1993), p. 156.
9. Jeffrey Solow, videotape, "Physically Efficient Cello Playing," from MedArt International 1992 World Congress on Arts and Medicine.

Chapter 11: Spontaneous Insight

1. For information about *jo ha kyu,* I am indebted to Arawana Hayashi, Irene Johansen, and the book *On the Art of the Nō Drama: The Major Treatises of Zeami,* translated by J. Thomas Rimer and Yamazaki Masakazu (Princeton, N.J.: Princeton University Press, 1984).
2. Ralph Kirkpatrick, "Preface" to *Sixty Sonatas,* by Domenico Scarlatti, vol. I (New York: G. Schirmer, 1953), p. xv.
3. Edward E. Lowinsky, "On Mozart's Rhythm," in *The Creative World of Mozart,* edited by Paul Henry Lang (New York: W.W. Norton & Co., 1963), pp. 35–37.

Chapter 13: Playing by Heart

1. Alexander Libermann, *A Comprehensive Approach to the Piano* (Berkeley, Calif.: Arif Press, 1984), pp. 9–10.

Chapter 14: Generosity

1. Diane Nichols, "The Demons Within: Confronting Performance Anxiety," *Chamber Music Magazine,* December 1995, pp. 20–40.

Recommended Reading

The Anatomy Coloring Book, by Wynn Kapit and Lawrence M. Elson. New York: HarperCollins, 1977.

The Art of Calligraphy: Joining Heaven and Earth, by Chögyam Trungpa. Boston: Shambhala Publications, 1994.

The Art of Quartet Playing: The Guarneri Quartet in Conversation with David Blum, by David Blum. Ithaca, N.Y.: Cornell University Press, 1986.

Back Trouble: A New Approach to Prevention and Recovery, by Deborah Caplan, P.T. Gainesville, Fla.: Triad Publishing Co., 1987.

"The Demons Within: Confronting Performance Anxiety," by Diane Nichols. *Chamber Music Magazine,* December 1995.

Dharma Art, by Chögyam Trungpa. Boston: Shambhala Publications, 1996.

Freedom to Learn, by Carl Rogers. New York: Macmillan, 1994.

Goodbye to Bad Backs: Stretching and Strengthening Exercises for Alignment and Freedom from Lower Back Pain, by Judith Scott. Pennington, N.J.: Princeton Book Co., 1988.

The Healing Forces of Music: History, Theory and Practice, by Randall McClellan, Ph.D. Amity, N.Y.: Amity House, Inc., 1988.

How to Learn the Alexander Technique: A Manual for Students, by Barbara Conable and William Conable. Columbus, Ohio: Andover Road Press, 1992.

A Musician's Survival Guide: A Guide to Preventing and Treating Injuries in Instrumentalists, by Richard Norris, M.D. St. Louis, Mo.: International Conference of Symphony and Opera Musicians, MMB Music, Inc., 1993.

"On Mozart's Rhythm," by Edward E. Lowinsky. In *The Creative World of Mozart,* edited by Paul Henry Lang. New York: W.W. Norton and Co., 1963.

"Performance," from the Preface by Ralph Kirkpatrick to *Sixty Sonatas* by Domenico Scarlatti. New York: G. Schirmer, 1953.

"Physically Efficient Cello Playing," by Jeffrey Solow. In *Current Research in Arts and Medicine: A Compendium of the MedArt International 1992 World Congress on Arts and Medicine,* edited by Fadi J. Bejjani, M.D., Ph.D. Pennington, N.J.: a cappella books, 1993.

The Physiological Mechanics of Piano Technique, by Otto Ortmann. New York: E.P. Dutton & Co., 1962.

The Pianist's Talent: A New Approach to Piano Playing Based on the Principles of F. Matthias Alexander and Raymond Thiberge, by Harold Taylor. New York: Taplinger Publishing Co., 1979.

Repetitive Strain Injury: A Computer User's Guide, by Emil Pascarelli, M.D., and Deborah Quilter. New York: John Wiley & Sons, Inc., 1994.

Rhythm and Movement: Applications of Dalcroze Eurhythmics, by Elsa R. Findlay. Evanston, Ill.: Summy-Birchard, 1971.

Self-Transformation Through Music, by Joanne Crandall. Wheaton, Ill.: Quest Books, 1986.

Shambhala: The Sacred Path of the Warrior, by Chögyam Trungpa. Boston: Shambhala Publications, 1988.

A Soprano on Her Head: Right-side-up Reflections on Life and Other Performances, by Eloise Ristad. Moab, Utah: Real People Press, 1982.

Structural Hearing: Tonal Coherence in Music, by Felix Salzer. New York: Dover Publications, 1962.

The Supple Body: The Way to Fitness, Strength, and Flexibility, by Sara Black. New York: Macmillan, 1995.

Tone Deaf and All Thumbs? An Invitation to Music Making, by Frank R. Wilson. New York: Vintage Books, 1987.

You Are Your Instrument: The Definitive Musician's Guide to Practice and Performance, by Julie Lyonn Lieberman. New York: Huiksi Music, 1991.

Resources for Musicians

Meditation Instruction

Private meditation instruction in the Buddhist and Shambhala traditions and group meditation and study programs are available at Shambhala Centers in the United States, Canada, and Europe.

To locate a center near you, contact
Shambhala International
1084 Tower Road
Halifax, Nova Scotia B3H 2Y5
Canada
(902) 425-4275

Arts Medicine Services

To locate a performing arts medicine clinic or referral service near you, contact
The International Arts Medicine Association
3600 Market Street
Philadelphia, PA 19104
(610) 525-3784

Bodywork Methods

The Alexander Technique cultivates an awareness of body use and the ability to differentiate between necessary and unnecessary effort. Through verbal and hands-on guidance, the student learns to carry out such daily activities as sitting, standing, bending, reaching, lifting, walking, and working at a computer with ease. Musicians also learn to free themselves from inefficient and tension-producing postural and movement habits in practicing their instruments and experience increased freedom in making music. The technique focuses particularly on releasing tension in the neck, maintaining a lengthened and well-aligned spine, and releasing the joints to discover natural coordination and grace.

To locate a certified teacher, contact

The North American Society of
   Teachers of the Alexander Technique
P.O. Box 3992
Champaign, IL 61826
(800) 473-0620

The Feldenkrais Method® enhances awareness and fine-tunes movement patterns in two ways: Functional Integration® uses slow, gentle touch in private sessions to guide the student through a series of movements that reeducate the neuromuscular system and result in improved movement habits and increased range of motion. In much of the work the student lies comfortably on a table, or sits in a chair, and becomes familiar with primitive reflexes and neurodevelopmental patterns that form the basis of healthy functioning. Awareness Through Movement® takes place in a classroom setting. While sitting, standing, or lying down, students are verbally guided through sequences of light, effortless movements and develop an awareness of bodily changes as they learn to move with greater ease and efficiency. Musicians may also work with their instruments in Feldenkrais sessions.

To locate a teacher, contact

The Feldenkrais Guild
P.O. Box 489
Albany, OR 97321
(541) 926-0981

The Rosen Method uses gentle, yet firm, touch and verbal interaction in a quiet, supportive environment to explore how muscle tension and restricted breathing are adaptive responses to life's experiences. Increased body awareness, relaxation, and reexperiencing of emotions and needs that have been held down or back results in more aliveness, spontaneity, and power in performance and in daily life.

To locate a practitioner, call
(203) 319-1090

Laban Movement Analysis (LMA) addresses both the functional and expressive aspects of movement. The LMA-trained practitioner (known as a Certified Movement Analyst, or CMA) works with the student to expand his or her movement repertoire by developing a balance between exertion and recuperation and between stability and mobility. The work also explores contrasting movement experiences such as delicacy and strength; sustainment and quickness; and vertical, horizontal, sagittal, diagonal, and circular movement. The CMA looks at how the body changes shape in motion and works with the student's inner impulses to move and attitude toward flow, weight, time, and space.

CMA's are also trained in the following:

Bartenieff Fundamentals (BF), which focuses on use of breath, intentionality, effective weight shift, body part relationships, spatial awareness, and perceptual-motor development in adults and children.

Laban/Bartenieff sessions for musicians are conducted with and without the student's instrument.

Laban Movement Analysis (LMA), Bartenieff Fundamentals (BF), and Certified Movement Analyst (CMA) are service marks of the Laban/Bartenieff Institute of Movement Studies.

To locate a practitioner, contact
Association of Laban Movement Analysts
c/o Laban/Bartenieff Institute of Movement Studies
11 East 4th Street
New York, NY 10003
(212) 477-4299

Body-Mind Centering® (BMC), like Laban Movement Analysis, offers a multifaceted approach to movement reeducation through an experiential study of how the mind—e.g., idea, intention, emotion—is expressed through the body in movement. BMC explores how the major body systems—skeletal, muscular, organic, nervous, glandular, and fluid—affect movement and aims to enhance healthy patterns in neuromuscular functioning by identifying the particular dynamics that underlie potentially injurious movement habits. Like Bartenieff

Fundamentals, BMC works with principles of developmental movement. The work encourages the student to explore stages of early childhood movement that may have been skipped so that he or she can correct movement problems at their root level. Musicians may work with their instruments at BMC sessions.

To locate a certified teacher, contact
The Body-Mind Centering Association
16 Center Street, Suite 530
Northampton, MA 01060
(413) 582-3617

Embodiment Education integrates Body-Mind Centering® with Laban Movement Analysis, sensory awareness, and Buddhist psychology to coordinate and fine-tune perception, movement, and emotion. Through hands-on therapy, postural-movement analysis, perceptual and movement exercises, and verbal interaction, the student develops awareness, releases habitual patterns of tension and misuse, and liberates emotional energy. This process guides a musician toward a more uplifted, relaxed yet energetic, and wholehearted approach to music-making. Sessions are conducted with and without the student's instrument.

This method is currently taught only by
Joan Campbell Whitacre, M.A.
685 West End Avenue, #12D
New York, NY 10025
(212) 662-8408

Somatic Movement Therapy Training blends Laban Movement Analysis, Body-Mind Centering®, and Bartenieff Fundamentals, affording in-depth assessment and individually tailored interventions.

To locate a practitioner, contact
Moving On Center
The School for Participatory Arts and Research (SPAR)
1428 Alice Street
Oakland, CA 94612
(510) 834-0284

Music Teachers and Health Professionals Interviewed for This Book

Dr. Fadi J. Bejjani
University Rehabilitation Associates
90 Bergen Street, Suite 3300
Newark, NJ 07103-2499
(201) 982-2802

Stephen Burns, solo trumpeter, Professor of Music
Indiana University School of Music
Bloomington, IN 47401
(812) 855-5421

Deborah Caplan, physical therapist and
    Certified Teacher of the Alexander Technique, N.A.S.T.A.T.
365 West End Avenue, #13C
New York, NY 10023
(212) 724-1372

James Carson, voice teacher
523 West 112th Street, #81
New York NY 10025
(212) 865-3066

Robert Cohen, Certified Teacher of the Alexander Technique,
    N.A.S.T.A.T.
408 West 36th Street, #3F
New York, NY 10018
(212) 643-9322

Martha Eddy, Certified Movement Analyst, Certified Teacher of
    Body-Mind Centering, Registered Movement Therapist
Director of Somatic Movement Therapy Training
Moving On Center
1428 Alice Street
Oakland, CA 94612
(510) 834-0284

Dr. Patrick Fazzari
Department of Rehabilitation Medicine
Roosevelt Hospital
1000 Tenth Avenue
New York, NY 10019
(212) 523-6597

Caryl Johnson, hand therapist
Hand Surgery Suite
Roosevelt Hospital
1000 Tenth Avenue
New York, NY 10019
(212) 523-7599

Jeannette Lovetri, voice teacher
Director of the Voice Workshop
c/o 317 West 93rd Street, #3B
New York, NY 10025
(718) 965-0624

Frances Magnes, violinist
Faculty, Hoff-Barthelson Music School
25 School Lane
Scarsdale, NY 10583
(914) 723-1169

Hope Martin, Certified Teacher of the Alexander Technique,
N.A.S.T.A.T.
15 East 17th Street, 6th Floor
New York, NY 10003
(212) 243-3867

Melanie Nevis, percussionist (Afro-Caribbean, rock, pop, world
music) and Certified Teacher of the Alexander Technique,
N.A.S.T.A.T.
c/o Lucy Moses School of Music and Dance
129 West 67th Street
New York, NY 10023
(212) 645-1479

Diane Nichols, M.S.W., psychotherapist
Director, Performing Arts Psychotherapy Center
111 West 57th Street, Suite 1422
New York, NY 10019
(212) 932-9201

Patrick O'Brien, guitarist/lutenist
106 West 28th Street
New York, NY 10001
(718) 783-6791

Dr. Emil Pascarelli
16 East 60th Street
New York, NY 10022
(212) 326-3348

Karen Ritscher, violist
Faculty, Manhattan School of Music and Mannes College of Music
241 West 97th Street, #13M
New York, NY 10025
(212) 222-3067

Dr. Mark Seem, acupuncturist
Director, Tri-State Institute of Traditional Chinese Acupuncture
20 West 86th Street
New York, NY 10024
(212) 496-7869

James Wang, physical therapist
336 Central Park West, #1F
New York, NY 10025
(212) 961-0353

Janet Weiss, flutist
163 Lake Shore Drive
Oakland, NJ 07436
(201) 337-9180

Joan Campbell Whitacre, M.A., Certified Teacher of Body-Mind
    Centering® Registered Movement Therapist, Authorized
    Meditation Instructor in the Buddhist tradition, teacher of
    Embodiment Education
685 West End Avenue, #12D
New York, NY 10025
(212) 662-8408

Joni Yecalsik, Iyengar yoga teacher
417 East 9th Street, #13
New York, NY 10009
(212) 673-3227

Rhythm and Dance Training

Dalcroze Eurhythmics
To locate a class or teacher training program near you, contact
    Leslie Mills
    Dalcroze Society of America
    390 Riverside Drive, #7G
    New York, NY 10025
    or call (800) 471-0012

Baroque Dance Classes (California)
A two-week summer workshop, with separate classes for beginning,
intermediate, and advanced students. Study includes notation and re-
constructing a dance to music.
    Contact
    Music Department
    The Braun Music Center
    Stanford University
    Stanford, CA 94305-3076
    (415) 723-3811
    Contact college music departments in your area to inquire about
other possible classes or workshops in baroque dance.

Rhythm Training Through Percussion (New York City)
Classes for nonpercussionists to improve their rhythmic skills on their

instruments. Emphasis on good body use through principles of the Alexander Technique.

Contact
Melanie Nevis
c/o Lucy Moses School of Music and Dance
129 West 67th Street
New York, NY 10023
(212) 645-1479

Creative Process: The Art of Making a True Move (Boston area)
Workshops with Arawana Hayashi, director of the Jo Ha Kyu Performance Group.

These workshops are directed toward both dancers and "nondancers" who want to uncover and nurture their innate creativity by means of a meditative discipline. The work demands a precise and intimate attention to the moving body but also reveals that stillness and space are equally important in expressing one's natural musicality. The exercises and forms presented in the workshop allow each person to discover his or her own creative process. This process brings clarity and a sense of richness to everyday life as well as to formal artistic endeavors.

For information call (617) 782-5352.

About the Author

Christian Steiner

Pianist Madeline Bruser has performed as soloist with the San Francisco and Denver Symphony Orchestras. She has conducted seminars and workshops on the Art of Practicing at the Juilliard School, the Manhattan School of Music, the MedArt World Congress on Arts and Medicine, Steinway Hall, and college music departments and music teachers' organizations in the United States and Canada. She has also taught teacher-training workshops at American and Canadian music schools. Ms. Bruser lives with her husband and daughter in New York City, where she teaches privately and conducts regular seminars and teacher-training programs. Her Web site address is www.artofpracticing.com.

Other Bell Tower Books

*Books that nourish the soul, illuminate the mind,
and speak directly to the heart*

Valeria Alfeyeva
PILGRIMAGE TO DZHVARI
A Woman's Journey of Spiritual Awakening
An unforgettable introduction to the riches of the
Eastern Orthodox mystical tradition. A modern *Way of a Pilgrim.*
0-517-88389-9 Softcover

Melody Ermachild Chavis
ALTARS IN THE STREET
A Story of Courage, Community, and Spiritual Awakening
A beautifully written memoir that captures
the essence of human struggles and resourcefulness.
0-609-80196-1 Softcover

Tracy Cochran and Jeff Zaleski
TRANSFORMATIONS
Awakening to the Sacred in Ourselves
An exploration of enlightenment experiences and
the ways in which they can transform our lives.
0-517-70150-2 Hardcover

David A. Cooper
ENTERING THE SACRED MOUNTAIN
Exploring the Mystical Practices of Judaism, Buddhism, and Sufism
An inspiring chronicle of one man's search for truth.
0-517-88464-X Softcover

Marc David
NOURISHING WISDOM
A Mind/Body Approach to Nutrition and Well-Being
A book that advocates awareness in eating.
0-517-88129-2 Softcover

Kat Duff
THE ALCHEMY OF ILLNESS
A luminous inquiry into the function and purpose of illness.
0-517-88097-0 Softcover

Joan Furman, MSN, RN, and David McNabb
THE DYING TIME
Practical Wisdom for the Dying and Their Caregivers
A comprehensive guide, filled with physical,
emotional, and spiritual advice.
0-609-80003-5 Softcover

Bernard Glassman
BEARING WITNESS
A Zen Master's Lessons in Making Peace
How Glassman started the Zen Peacemaker Order and
what each of us can do to make peace in our hearts and in the world.
0-609-60061-3 Hardcover

Bernard Glassman and Rick Fields
INSTRUCTIONS TO THE COOK
A Zen Master's Lessons in Living a Life That Matters
A distillation of Zen wisdom that can be used equally well as
a manual on business or spiritual practice, cooking or life.
0-517-88829-7 Softcover

Burghild Nina Holzer
A WALK BETWEEN HEAVEN AND EARTH
A Personal Journal on Writing and the Creative Process
How keeping a journal focuses and expands our awareness of
ourselves and everything that touches our lives.
0-517-88096-2 Softcover

Greg Johanson and Ron Kurtz
GRACE UNFOLDING
Psychotherapy in the Spirit of the Tao-te ching
The interaction of client and therapist illuminated through the
gentle power and wisdom of Lao Tsu's ancient classic.
0-517-88130-6 Softcover

Selected by Marcia and Jack Kelly
ONE HUNDRED GRACES
Mealtime Blessings
A collection of graces from many traditions, inscribed in calligraphy
reminiscent of the manuscripts of medieval Europe.
0-517-58567-7 Hardcover
0-609-80093-0 Softcover

Jack and Marcia Kelly
SANCTUARIES
*A Guide to Lodgings in Monasteries, Abbeys,
and Retreats of the United States*
For those in search of renewal and a little peace; described by the
New York Times as "the *Michelin Guide* of the retreat set."
THE NORTHEAST 0-517-57727-5 Softcover
THE COMPLETE U.S. 0-517-88517-4 Softcover

Marcia M. Kelly
HEAVENLY FEASTS
Memorable Meals from Monasteries, Abbeys, and Retreats
Delectable repasts savored by the Kellys on their travels.
0-517-88522-0 Softcover

Marcia and Jack Kelly
THE WHOLE HEAVEN CATALOG
*A Resource Guide to Products, Services, Arts, Crafts, and Festivals
of Religious, Spiritual, and Cooperative Communities*
All the things that monks and nuns do to support their habits!
0-609-80120-1 Softcover

Barbara Lachman
THE JOURNAL OF HILDEGARD OF BINGEN
A year in the life of the twelfth-century German saint—
the diary she never had the time to write herself.
0-517-59169-3 Hardcover
0-517-88390-2 Softcover

Katharine Le Mée
CHANT
The Origins, Form, Practice, and
Healing Power of Gregorian Chant
The ways in which this ancient liturgy can nourish us
and transform our lives.
0-517-70037-9 Hardcover

Stephen Levine
A YEAR TO LIVE
How to Live This Year as if It Were Your Last
Using the consciousness of our mortality
to enter into a new and vibrant relationship with life.
0-609-80194-5 Softcover

Gunilla Norris
BEING HOME
A Book of Meditations
An exquisite modern book of hours, a celebration
of mindfulness in everyday activities.
0-517-58159-0 Hardcover

Marcia Prager
THE PATH OF BLESSING
Experiencing the Energy and Abundance of the Divine
How to use the traditional Jewish practice of calling down a
blessing on each action as a profound path of spiritual growth.
0-517-70363-7 Hardcover

271